THE PSALMS

A New Translation for Worship

Glory to the Father and | to the | Son:
and | to the | Holy | Spirit;
as it was in the be|ginning · is | now:
and shall be for | ever | A|men.

THE PSALMS

A New Translation for Worship

POINTED FOR SINGING TO
ANGLICAN CHANT

Published in cooperation with
CHURCH INFORMATION OFFICE by
COLLINS

Collins Liturgical Publications
187 Piccadilly, London W1V 9DA

First published 1977

ISBN 0 00 599546 9 (cased edition)
ISBN 0 00 599584 1 (limp edition)

Made and printed in Great Britain
by Richard Clay (The Chaucer Press) Ltd
Bungay, Suffolk

CONTENTS

THE TRANSLATORS

Hebrew Panel

Sebastian P. Brock, M.A., D.Phil., University Lecturer in Aramaic and Syriac, and Fellow of Wolfson College, Oxford. (Church of England)

The Rev. J. A. Emerton, M.A., D.D. (*Chairman*), Regius Professor of Hebrew, and Fellow of St John's College, Cambridge. (Church of England)

The Rev. William Horbury, M.A., Ph.D., Vicar of Great Gransden; formerly Fellow of Clare College, Cambridge; Examining Chaplain to the Bishop of Peterborough. (Church of England)

The Rev. John F. McHugh, L.S.S., Ph.L., S.T.D., Lecturer in Theology, University of Durham; formerly Director of Studies and Lecturer in Sacred Scripture at Ushaw College, Durham. (Roman Catholic)

The Rev. A. A. Macintosh, M.A. (*Secretary*), Fellow, Tutor and Assistant Dean of St John's College, Cambridge; Examining Chaplain to the Bishop of Carlisle. (Church of England)

The Rev. A. G. MacLeod, M.A., Principal of Westminster College, Cambridge; formerly Moderator of the Presbyterian Church of England. (United Reformed Church)

The Rev. Ernest W. Nicholson, M.A., B.D., Ph.D., University Lecturer in Divinity, and Fellow and Dean of Pembroke College, Cambridge. (Church of England)

John G. Snaith, M.A., B.D., University Lecturer in Hebrew and Aramaic, Cambridge; Member of the Faith and Order Committee of the Methodist Church; Local Preacher. (Methodist)

English

David L. Frost, M.A., Ph.D., Professor of English, University of Newcastle, New South Wales; formerly Fellow of St John's College, Cambridge; member of the Church of England Liturgical Commission. (Church of England)

The pointing of the Psalms was done by

Roy Massey, B.Mus., Organist and Master of the Choristers, Hereford Cathedral.

Lionel Dakers, B.Mus., Director of the Royal School of Church Music.

The Rev. Canon Cyril V. Taylor, M.A., formerly Precentor of Salisbury Cathedral.

INTRODUCTION

THE PSALMS

Christians have used the Psalms in their praises of God, in their prayers and in their meditations since the earliest days of the Church. The Jews have used the Psalms for a much longer time, for they were composed for use in ancient Israel. The majority of the Psalms are hymns of praise and thanksgiving to God for what he is and for what he has done (e.g. Pss. 8, 104, 135), or prayers for help and laments because of the sufferings of an individual (e.g. Pss. 6, 22) or his anxieties (e.g. Ps. 77), or because of some national disaster such as defeat in battle (e.g. Ps. 44) or the destruction of Jerusalem and its temple (e.g. Pss. 74, 79). There are also meditations on God's providence (e.g. Pss. 49, 73, 78) or on his commandments (e.g. Pss. 1, 119). Other Psalms were composed for particular occasions in the nation's life: for the accession of a new king (Ps. 2), for a royal wedding (Ps. 45), or for a pilgrimage to Jerusalem to worship at the temple (e.g. Pss. 84, 122). The temple was the place where most Psalms were originally intended to be sung, but they also came to be used by Jewish congregations in their synagogues and by individuals in their private prayers.

The period in which Psalms were composed in ancient Israel goes back as early as the time of King David (*c.* 1000 BC), though modern scholars have questioned the tradition that he was the author of a large number of the poems in our Psalter. Some Psalms were certainly written much later: Ps. 137, for instance, speaks of the exile of the Jews from Jerusalem to Babylon in the sixth century BC. Most of the Psalms, however, cannot be dated precisely and might have been written at almost any time within a period of several centuries. Nor do we know when the last poem in the Psalter was written, though it was probably not later than about 200 BC and may well have been much earlier. The Psalms thus reflect something like three quarters of a millennium in the life and worship of ancient Israel.

Jesus was born a Jew, and he was brought up to know the Psalms intimately and to ponder them. He quoted them in his teaching, and words from the Psalter were on his lips as he hung on the cross. The Church learned from him, and from God's ancient people the Jews, to value the Psalms, and Christians have used them ever since.

When Christians read the Psalms, they meditate and share the thoughts and varied emotions of the people of God in the Old Testament, the people to whom God made himself known, and they share in Israel's experience of God. The God of the Psalms is the God and Father of our Lord Jesus Christ. The coming of Christ has, however, made a difference, and Christians cannot always think of God in exactly the same way as those who lived before the birth, and death, and resurrection of Jesus. Christians cannot make their own everything in the Psalter, at least not in its original sense. We cannot, for example, identify ourselves with the author of Ps. 137 when he blesses those who will dash Babylonian children against the rocks, however well we may understand the Psalmist's reaction to the murder by Babylonian soldiers of Jewish children. There are parts of the Psalter that Christians must read with detachment. Many Christians feel that they must go further and refrain from the use of such passages, at least in public worship. Nevertheless, although there are verses in the Psalter whose sentiments Christians must not share, there remains much more which they can wholeheartedly make their own.

Throughout the centuries, Christians of different persuasions have found the Psalms a means of prayer and worship that fulfilled their needs. In the future, as in the past, Christians will use the Psalms both in the public worship of the Church and in their private devotions, in meditation, in prayer, and, above all, in praise.

THE NEW TRANSLATION

This present translation was made primarily, though not exclusively, for public worship. Miles Coverdale's version of the Psalms in the Book of Common Prayer has been used for more than four hundred years, and it is well loved by many Anglicans (not least by the members of the translation panel). It will doubtless continue to be used. Yet there are two reasons why a new translation was necessary. First, the Psalms were written in Hebrew, and the study of the Hebrew language and the textual problems of the Old Testament has advanced considerably in the past century, and even in recent years. More is known about the meanings of the Hebrew words and the history of the text of the Hebrew Bible, and techniques have been developed for dealing with obscure passages and verses where it is likely that mistakes were made by scribes copying the text by hand in ancient times. Second, there was a need for a translation that would express the meaning clearly in modern English in a style suitable for use in public worship. There have been several new translations in recent years, but the present one is intended primarily for public speaking and singing.

In September 1970 the Church of England Liturgical Commission invited one of its members, Dr (now Professor) David Frost, to begin work on a liturgical Psalter suitable for use in the services in modern English that the Commission was in process of preparing. At that early stage it was hoped to produce such a Psalter by modestly revising Coverdale's version in the Book of Common Prayer by reference to other English versions (both old and new) and, where it was thought necessary, to the Hebrew Bible. A revision of Coverdale's version had, indeed, earlier been undertaken for the Church of England at the request of the then Archbishops of Canterbury and York and published by the S.P.C.K. in 1963 as *The Revised Psalter*. The members of the Commission who prepared it have been justifiably praised for their skill in removing many errors and obscurities without losing the familiar flavour of the English of the Prayer Book. Yet their very success in achieving their purpose meant that the revised translation did not meet the needs of services in modern English.

As the work proceeded, it became clear that the projected Psalter could not be produced satisfactorily except on the basis of a fresh translation of the Hebrew original. At the same time, increasing interest in the project in this country and abroad, not only from Anglicans but also from members of other Churches, was reported to the Commission. Therefore, with the approval of the Archbishops of Canterbury and York, the Regius Professor of Hebrew in the University of Cambridge was invited in 1972 to convene a panel of Hebrew scholars drawn from various Churches to cooperate with Dr Frost in preparing a new translation of the Psalter.

In the mean time, the work done between 1970 and 1972 was published in 1973 by the Church Information Office under the title *Twenty-Five Psalms from a Modern Liturgical Psalter*, with the intention that critics should have an opportunity to judge what was now regarded as a pilot scheme of the project as a whole. The pilot scheme was the work of Dr David Frost in collaboration with the Rev. Andrew Macintosh. Their translation has been revised and incorporated in the present version of the Psalter.

The preparation of this new translation of the Psalter is thus part of the process of revising the services of the Church of England, but it is hoped that it will be found useful by other branches of the Anglican Communion and also by other Christians. The panel responsible for the translation included members of the Roman Catholic, Methodist, and United Reformed Churches, as well as Anglicans – and it may be added that the differences of Christian allegiance made no difference at all to the way in which the problems of translation were tackled. It is also hoped that the translation will be found useful for private prayer and study in addition to public worship.

The translation panel consisted of eight Hebrew and biblical scholars, whose task was to determine the meaning of the Hebrew text, and of Dr Frost, who was responsible for the English wording of the translation. Seven of the Hebrew scholars (of whom two are laymen) teach in universities, and the eighth is the vicar of a country parish.

The first step in preparing the translation was for one of the Hebrew scholars (not always the same one) to make a draft rendering of a Psalm, and for his draft to be discussed and revised by the others. The second draft thus reflected the judgement, not just of one scholar, but of a team of scholars with a specialised knowledge of Hebrew and the Old Testament – and experience showed how much more could be learned by working as a team. The aim at this stage was to produce a rendering that expressed the meaning as simply and clearly as possible, and no attempt was made to achieve an acceptable English style, let alone literary elegance. While the meaning of most parts of the Psalms is clear, there are some obscure passages (e.g. Ps. 87), and the panel did their best to find a meaningful translation. There are also places where good sense cannot be obtained from the Hebrew text, and where there is reason to believe that mistakes were made by scribes in ancient times. In such passages the panel felt free to make small corrections of the Hebrew text. However, they were reluctant to make changes except where there was no satisfactory alternative. They were also cautious about accepting many recent theories concerning new meanings of Hebrew words, which have not won general acceptance. A translation for use in church should display a cautious attitude both towards emendations of the text and towards new lexicographical theories.

The next stage was the responsibility of David Frost. He took the draft agreed by the Hebrew scholars and prepared a rendering in an English style and rhythm suitable for singing or reading aloud in church. His translation came back to the panel, who were free to criticise it if they believed it to misrepresent the meaning of the Hebrew, or if (which happened only very rarely) they were dissatisfied with the English wording. They did not themselves alter the translation, but asked David Frost to take it away and revise it himself and to bring the revision back to the panel. It was thus hoped, on the one hand, to gain the considered opinion of the team of Hebrew scholars and, on the other, to avoid the flatness of what has been described as 'committee English'.

Finally, a panel of musicians studied the translation and prepared the edition that is pointed for chanting. If the wording was, in their opinion, difficult to sing, they asked the translators to consider whether revision was possible.

This translation is a new rendering of the Hebrew into modern English, not a revision of an older version. However, novelty has not been sought for its own sake, and we have felt free to make use of many phrases from earlier translations. Further, we have followed the example of the great translators in the sixteenth and seventeenth centuries, in keeping close to the images and idioms of the original Hebrew. The English language has been regularly refreshed by the importation of elements from foreign cultures, not least from Hebraic culture through the wisdom of early translators of the Bible into English; and we have thought lively expressions modelled on the Hebrew to be poetically preferable to tired expressions and clichés drawn from the vernacular. Partly because it seems right that the Psalms in Christian worship should be recognised to be from ancient Israel, we have not avoided slight archaisms appropriate to the purposes of poetry. However, we have tested the intelligibility of our drafts, particularly on those who are unfamiliar with older English versions: if we have not attempted to speak in the tones of daily conversation we have made every effort to render the Psalms into language that the ordinary Christian can understand.

Because we have been creating a literary version for public recitation and singing, we have not felt ourselves bound in all places to the strict letter of the Hebrew text, though we have translated the meaning of the whole as well as we were able. On occasion, to give singers sufficient syllables to sing, we have added one or two words to a half-verse, but these have always been justifiable expansions of the meaning of the Hebrew. Again, we have at times put 'God' instead of 'the Lord', or expanded a phrase so that it flows more smoothly: for instance, instead of beginning a Psalm with 'O God', we may begin 'O Lord our God'. Where a Hebrew phrase was obscure if translated baldly we have sometimes added an explanatory word, or offered a paraphrase or a double translation to convey the full meaning in English. Throughout, we have felt free to renumber and redivide the verses where that seemed required by the structure of the verse in English translation, but we have kept to the parallelism of Hebrew poetry and observed most of those divisions into half-lines indicated by Jewish tradition.

Some verses in this translation of the Psalms are printed in square brackets, so that they may be omitted by those who believe their contents to be unsuitable for use in public worship. Most of the bracketed verses are those that were bracketed in the 1928 Prayer Book, but a few changes have been made.

NOTES ON THE POINTING

1. Breath is to be taken at asterisks, and at the end of lines except when the pointing clearly forbids it, or when the sign ‿ is used to indicate a 'carry-over'.

A shorter break, or 'mental comma', made without taking breath, is indicated by an extra space between words.

2. The dot indicates how the syllables within a bar are to be divided, when there are more than two.

3. The sign † indicates use of the second half of a double chant.

4. A double space between verses indicates that a change of chant is appropriate.

5. The final '-ed' is to be pronounced as a separate syllable only when marked with an accent (e.g. blessèd).

6. Verses enclosed within square brackets may be omitted.

7. The Jewish doxologies which conclude Books 1 to 4 of the Psalter (see Psalms 41, 72, 89, 106) are enclosed within round brackets. When a Christian doxology is used, they may be omitted.

THE PSALMS

1

1 Blessèd is the man‿
who has not walked in the counsel | of the · un-| godly:
nor followed the way of sinners
nor taken his | seat a|mongst the | scornful.

2 But his delight is in the | law · of the | Lord:
and on that law will he | ponder | day and | night.

3 He is like a tree planted beside | streams of | water:
that yields its | fruit in | due | season.

4 Its leaves also | shall not | wither:
and look what|ever · he | does · it shall | prosper.

5 As for the ungodly * it is not | so with | them:
they are like the | chaff · which the | wind | scatters.

6 Therefore the ungodly shall not stand | up · at the | judgement:
nor sinners in the congre|gation | of the | righteous.

†7 For the Lord cares for the | way · of the | righteous:
but the | way of · the un|godly · shall | perish.

2

1 Why are the | nations · in | tumult:
and why do the peoples | cherish · a | vain | dream?

2 The kings of the earth rise up
and the rulers con|spire to|gether:
against the Lord and a|gainst · his an|ointed | saying,

†3 'Let us break their | bonds a|sunder:
let us throw | off their | chains | from us.'

4 He that dwells in heaven shall | laugh them · to | scorn:
the Lord will | hold them | in de|rision.

5 Then will he speak to them in his wrath
and terrify them | in his | fury:
'I the Lord have set up my king on | Zion · my | holy | hill.'

6 I will announce the Lord's decree
that which | he has | spoken:
'You are my son this | day have | I be|gotten you.

7 'Ask of me
and I will give you the nations for | your in|herit-ance:
the uttermost parts of the | earth for | your pos|session.

†8 'You shall break them with a | rod of | iron:
and shatter them in | pieces · like a | potter's | vessel.'

9 Now therefore be | wise O | kings:
be advised you that are | judges | of the | earth.

10 Serve the Lord with awe
and govern yourselves in | fear and | trembling:
lest he be angry and you | perish | in your | course.

†11 For his wrath is | quickly | kindled:
blessèd are those that | turn to | him for | refuge.

3

1 Lord how numerous ˈ are my ˈ enemies:
many they ˈ are that ˈ rise aˈgainst me.

2 Many there are that ˈ talk of me · and ˈ say:
'There is no ˈ help for · him ˈ in his ˈ God.'

3 But you Lord are about me ˈ as a ˈ shield:
you are my glory and the ˈ lifter ˈ up · of my ˈ head.

4 I cry to the Lord with a ˈ loud ˈ voice:
and he answers me ˈ from his ˈ holy ˈ hill.

5 I lay myself ˈ down and ˈ sleep:
I wake again beˈcause the ˈ Lord susˈtains me.

6 Therefore I will not be afraid‿
of the multitudes ˈ of the ˈ nations:
who have set themselves aˈgainst me · on ˈ every ˈ
side.

7 Arise Lord and deliver me ˈ O my ˈ God:
for you will strike all my enemies upon the cheek
you will ˈ break the ˈ teeth of · the unˈgodly.

8 Deliverance beˈlongs · to the ˈ Lord:
O let your ˈ blessing · be upˈon your ˈ people.

4

1 Answer me when I call O ǀ God of · my ǀ righteousness:
when I was hard-pressed you set me free
be gracious to me ǀ now and ǀ hear my ǀ prayer.

2 Sons of men how long will you turn my ǀ glory · to my ǀ shame:
how long will you love what is worthless
and ǀ seek ǀ after ǀ lies?

3 Know that the Lord has shown me his ǀ wonder·ful ǀ kindness:
when I call to the ǀ Lord ǀ he will ǀ hear me.

4 Tremble and ǀ do no ǀ sin:
commune with your own heart upǀon your ǀ bed · and be ǀ still.

5 Offer the sacrifices ǀ that are ǀ right:
and ǀ put your ǀ trust · in the ǀ Lord.

6 There are many who say 'Who will ǀ show us · any ǀ good?:
the light of your countenance O ǀ Lord has ǀ gone ǀ from us.'

7 Yet you have given my ǀ heart more ǀ gladness:
than they have when their corn ǀ wine and ǀ oil inǀcrease.

8 In peace I will lie ǀ down and ǀ sleep:
for you alone Lord ǀ make me ǀ dwell in ǀ safety.

5

1 Hear my words O Lord give ˈ heed · to my ˈ groaning:
listen to my cry you that are my ˈ king ˈ and my ˈ God.

2 In the morning when I pray to you
surely you will ˈ hear my ˈ voice:
at daybreak I lay my prayers beˈfore you · and ˈ look ˈ up.

3 For you are not a God who takes ˈ pleasure · in ˈ wickedness:
nor can any ˈ evil ˈ dwell with ˈ you.

4 The boastful cannot ˈ stand in · your ˈ sight:
you hate all ˈ those that ˈ work ˈ mischief.

5 Those who speak ˈ lies · you desˈtroy:
you abhor the treacherous O Lord
and ˈ those · that are ˈ stained with ˈ blood.

6 But because of your great goodness‿
I will ˈ come into · your ˈ house:
I will bow down toward your holy ˈ‿
temple · in ˈ awe and ˈ fear of you.

7 Lead me O Lord in your righteousness
for my enemies ˈ lie in ˈ wait:
make ˈ straight your ˈ way beˈfore me.

8 For there is no ˈ truth · in their ˈ mouth:
and within they are ˈ eaten ˈ up by ˈ malice.

9 Their throat is an ˈ open ˈ sepulchre:
and their tongue speaks ˈ smooth and ˈ flatter·ing ˈ words.

10 Destroy them O God * let them fall by their ˡ own con'triving:
cast them out for their many offences
for ˡ they have · re'belled a'gainst you.

11 But let all who put their trust in ˡ you re'joice:
let them ˡ shout with ˡ joy for ˡ ever.

12 Be the defender of those who ˡ love your ˡ name:
let them ex'ult be'cause of ˡ you.

†13 For you will bless O Lord the ˡ man · that is ˡ righteous:
you will cover him with your ˡ favour ˡ as · with a ˡ shield.

6

1 O Lord rebuke me not in your ˡ indig'nation:
nor chasten me ˡ in your ˡ fierce dis'pleasure.

2 Have mercy upon me O Lord for ˡ I am ˡ weak:
O Lord heal me for my ˡ very ˡ bones · are a'fraid.

3 My soul also is ˡ greatly ˡ troubled:
and you Lord how ˡ long will ˡ you de'lay?

4 Turn again O Lord and de'liver · my ˡ soul:
O save me ˡ for your ˡ mercy's ˡ sake.

5 For in death ˡ no man · re'members you:
and who can ˡ give you ˡ thanks · from the ˡ grave?

6 I am wearied ˡ with my ˡ groaning:
every night I drown my bed with weeping
and ˡ water · my ˡ couch · with my ˡ tears.

†7 My eyes waste a|way for | sorrow:
they grow dim be|cause of | all my | enemies.

8 Away from me all | you that · do | evil:
for the Lord has | heard the | voice · of my | weeping.

9 The Lord has heard my | suppli|cation:
the | Lord · will re|ceive my | prayer.

†10 All my enemies shall be put to shame and | greatly · dis|mayed:
they shall turn back and be con|founded | in a | moment.

7

1 O Lord my God to you have I | come for | shelter:
save me from all who pursue me * O | save | and de|liver me,

2 Lest like lions they | tear my | throat:
lest they carry me | off and | none can | save me.

3 O Lord my God if I have | done · such a | thing:
if there is any | wicked·ness | on my | hands,

4 If I have repaid with evil him that | was my | friend:
or plundered my | enemy · with|out just | cause,

†5 Then let the enemy pursue me and | over|take me:
let him trample my life to the ground
and lay my | honour | in the | dust.

6 Arise O | Lord · in your | anger:
rise up in | wrath a|gainst my | adversaries.

7 Awake my God * you that or|dain | justice:
and let the assembly of the | peoples | gather · a|bout you;

8 Take your seat | high a|bove them:
and sit in judgement O | Lord | over · the | nations.

9 Judge for me O Lord according | to my | righteousness:
and | as · my in|tegrity · re|quires.

10 Let the wickedness of the ungodly cease but es|tablish · the | righteous:
for you try the very hearts and minds of | men‿O | righteous | God.

11 God is my | shield | over me:
he pre|serves the | true of | heart.

12 God is a | righteous | judge:
and God condemns | evil | every | day.

13 If a man does not turn he | whets his | sword:
he bends his | bow and | makes it | ready;

†14 He prepares the | instruments · of | death:
and makes his | arrows | darts of | fire.

15 See how the ungodly con|ceives | mischief:
how he swells with wickedness | and gives | birth to | lies.

16 He digs a pit and | hollows · it | out:
but falls himself into the | trap · he had | made for | others.

17 His mischief rebounds upon his ˡ own ˡ head:
and his violence comes ˡ down · on his ˡ own ˡ pate.

18 I will thank the ˡ Lord · for his ˡ justice:
I will sing ˡ praises · to the ˡ Lord Most ˡ High.

8

1 O ˡ Lord our ˡ Governor:
how glorious is your ˡ name in ˡ all the ˡ earth!

2 Your majesty above the heavens is ˡ yet reˡcounted:
by the ˡ mouths of ˡ babes and ˡ sucklings.

†3 You have founded a strong defence‿
aˡgainst your ˡ adversaries:
to quell the ˡ ene·my ˡ and · the aˡvenger.

4 When I consider your heavens the ˡ work of · your ˡ
fingers:
the moon and the stars which ˡ you have ˡ set in ˡ
order,

5 What is man that you should be ˡ mindful ˡ of him:
or the son of ˡ man that ˡ you should ˡ care for him?

6 Yet you have made him little ˡ less · than a ˡ god:
and have ˡ crowned him · with ˡ glory · and ˡ honour.

7 You have made him the ˡ master · of your ˡ handiwork:
and have put all things in subˡjection · beˡneath his ˡ
feet,

8 All ǀ sheep and ǀ oxen:
and all the ǀ creatures ǀ of the ǀ field,

9 The birds of the air and the ǀ fish · of the ǀ sea:
and everything that moves‿
in the pathways ǀ of the ǀ great ǀ waters.

†10 O ǀ Lord our ǀ Governor:
how glorious is your ǀ name in ǀ all the ǀ earth!

9

1 I will give you thanks O Lord with my ǀ whole ǀ heart:
I will tell of all the ǀ wonders ǀ you have ǀ done.

2 I will reǀjoice · and be ǀ glad in you:
I will make my songs to your ǀ name ǀ O Most ǀ High.

3 For my enemies are ǀ driven ǀ back:
they stumble and ǀ perish ǀ at your ǀ presence.

4 You have maintained my ǀ cause · and my ǀ right:
you sat enǀthroned · as a ǀ righteous ǀ judge.

5 You rebuked the heathen nations
you brought the ǀ wicked · to deǀstruction:
you blotted out their ǀ name for ǀ ever · and ǀ ever.

6 The strongholds of the enemy are made a perpetual ǀ
desoǀlation:
you plucked up their cities‿
and ǀ even · their ǀ memory · has ǀ perished.

7 The Lord confounds them * but the Lord en|dures for | ever:
he has | set up · his | throne for | judgement.

8 He shall judge the | world with | righteousness:
and deal true | justice | to the | peoples.

9 The Lord is a strong tower to | him that · is op|pressed:
he is a tower of | strength in | time of | need.

10 All who heed your name will | trust in | you:
for you have never for|saken | those that | seek you.

11 O sing praises to the Lord who | dwells in | Zion:
tell among the peoples what | great things | he has | done.

12 For he that avenges blood has re|membered · the | poor:
he has | not for|gotten · their | cry.

13 The Lord has been merciful toward me
he saw what I | suffered · from my | foes:
he raised me up a|gain · from the | gates of | death,

14 That I might tell all your praises in the | gates of | Zion:
that I might re|joice in | your de|liverance.

15 The nations have sunk into the pit they | dug for | others:
in the very snare they | laid · is their | foot | taken;

16 The Lord has declared himself and up|held the | right:
the wicked are trapped in the | work · of their | own | hands.

17 The wicked shall be given | over · to | death:
and all the nations | that for|get | God.

18 For the needy shall not always | be for|gotten:
nor shall the hope of the | poor | perish · for | ever.

19 Arise Lord let not | man pre|vail:
let the | nations · be | judged be|fore you.

20 Put them in | fear O | Lord:
and let the nations | know · that they | are but | men.

10

1 Why do you stand far | off O | Lord:
why do you hide your | face in | time of | need?

2 The ungodly in their pride | persecute · the | poor:
let them be caught in the | schemes they | have de|vised.

3 For the ungodly man boasts of his | heart's de|sire:
he grasps at profit he | spurns · and blas|phemes the | Lord.

4 He says in his arrogance | 'God will · not a|venge':
'There is no | God' is | all his | thought.

5 He is settled in | all his | ways:
your statutes O Lord are far above him | ‿ and he | does not | see.

6 He snorts defiance at his enemies
he says in his heart 'I shall | never · be | shaken:
I shall walk se|cure from | any · man's | curse.'

7 His mouth is full of op|pression · and de|ceit:
mischief and | wickedness · lie | under · his | tongue.

8 He skulks a|bout · in the | villages:
and | secret·ly | murders · the | innocent.

9 His eyes watch | out · for the | helpless:
he lurks con|cealed · like a | lion · in a | thicket.

10 He lies in wait to | seize up·on the | poor:
he lays hold on the poor man and | drags him | off · in his | net.

11 The upright are crushed and | humbled · be|fore him:
and the helpless | fall in|to his | power.

12 He says in his heart | 'God · has for|gotten:
he has covered his | face and | sees | nothing.'

13 Arise O Lord God lift | up your | hand:
for|get · not the | poor for | ever.

14 Why should the wicked man | spurn | God:
why should he say in his heart | 'He will | not a|venge'?

15 Surely you see the | trouble · and the | sorrow:
you look on and will take it | into · your | own | hands.

16 The helpless commits him|self to | you:
for you are the | helper | of the | fatherless.

†17 Break the | power of · the un|godly:
search out his wickedness | till · it is | found no | more.

18 The Lord is king for | ever · and | ever:
the heathen have | perished | from his | land.

19 You have heard the longing of the ˡ meek O ˡ Lord:
you turned your ˡ ear · to their ˡ hearts' deˡsire,

†20 To help the poor and fatherless ˡ to their ˡ right:
that men may no more be ˡ terri·fied ˡ from their ˡ land.

11

1 In the Lord I have ˡ found my ˡ refuge:
how then can you say to me ˡ
'Flee · like a ˡ bird · to the ˡ mountains;

2 'Look how the wicked bend their bows
and notch the arrow upˡon the ˡ string:
to shoot from the ˡ darkness · at the ˡ true of ˡ heart;

3 'If the foundations ˡ are desˡtroyed:
what ˡ can the ˡ just man ˡ do?'

4 The Lord is in his holy place
the Lord is enˡthroned in ˡ heaven:
his eyes search out
his glance ˡ tries the ˡ children · of ˡ men.

5 He tries the ˡ righteous · and the ˡ wicked:
and him that delights in ˡ violence · his ˡ soul abˡhors.

6 He will rain down coals of fire and brimstone‿
upˡon the ˡ wicked:
a scorching wind shall ˡ be their ˡ cup to ˡ drink.

†7 For the Lord is righteous and loves ˡ righteous ˡ acts:
the ˡ upright · shall ˡ see his ˡ face.

12

1 Help Lord for there is not one | godly · man | left:
the faithful have vanished from a|mong the | children · of | men.

2 Everyone tells | lies · to his | neighbour:
they flatter with their lips‿
but | speak · from a | double | heart.

3 If only the Lord would cut off all | flatter·ing | lips:
and the | tongue that | speaks so | proudly!

4 They say 'By our tongues we | shall pre|vail:
our lips are our servants who is | lord | over | us?'

5 Because of the oppression of the poor
because of the | groaning · of the | needy:
'I will arise' says the Lord
'and set them in safety from | those that | snarl | after them.'

6 The words of the Lord are pure
as silver re|fined · in a | crucible:
as gold that is seven times | puri·fied | in the | fire.

7 You will surely | guard us · O | Lord:
and shield us for ever from this | evil | gener|ation,

8 Though the ungodly strut on | every | side:
though the vilest of men have | master·y | of man|-kind.

13

1 How long O Lord will you so ˡ utterly · forˡget me:
how long will you ˡ hide your ˡ face ˡ from me?

2 How long must I suffer anguish in my soul
and be so grieved in my heart ˡ day and ˡ night:
how long shall my ˡ ene·my ˡ triumph ˡ over me?

3 Look upon me O Lord my ˡ God and ˡ answer me:
lighten my ˡ eyes · lest I ˡ sleep in ˡ death;

4 Lest my enemy say 'I have preˡvailed aˡgainst him':
lest my foes exˡult ˡ at my ˡ overthrow.

5 Yet I put my trust in your unˡfailing ˡ love:
O let my heart reˡjoice in ˡ your salˡvation.

6 And I will make my ˡ song · to the ˡ Lord:
because he ˡ deals so ˡ bounti·fully ˡ with me.

14

1 The fool has said in his heart 'There ˡ is no ˡ God':
they have all become vile and abominable in their doings there ˡ is not ˡ one that · does ˡ good.

2 The Lord looked down from heaven upon the ˡ children · of ˡ men:
to see if there were any who would act ˡ wisely · and ˡ seek · after ˡ God.

†3 But they have all turned out of the way
they have all alike be|come cor|rupt:
there is none that does | good | no not | one.

4 Are all the evildoers devoid of | under|standing:
who eat up my people as men eat bread‿
and | do not | pray · to the | Lord?

5 They shall be | struck with | terror:
for God is with the | compa·ny | of the | righteous.

6 Though they frustrate the poor man | in his | hopes:
surely the | Lord | is his | refuge.

7 O that deliverance for Israel might come | forth from | Zion:
when the Lord turns again the fortunes of his people
then shall Jacob re|joice and | Israel · be | glad.

15

1 Lord who may a|bide in · your | tabernacle:
or who may dwell up|on your | holy | hill?

2 He that leads an uncorrupt life
and does the | thing · which is | right:
who speaks the truth from his heart
and has not | slandered | with his | tongue;

3 He that has done no evil | to his | fellow:
nor vented a|buse a|gainst his | neighbour;

4 In whose eyes the worthless | have no | honour:
but he makes much of | those that | fear the | Lord;

5 He that has ǀ sworn · to his ǀ neighbour:
and will ǀ not go ǀ back · on his ǀ oath;

6 He that has not put his ǀ money · to ǀ usury:
nor taken a ǀ bribe aǀgainst the ǀ innocent.

†7 He that ǀ does these ǀ things:
shall ǀ never · be ǀ overǀthrown.

16

1 Preserve ǀ me O ǀ God:
for in ǀ you · have I ǀ taken ǀ refuge.

2 I have said to the Lord ǀ You are ǀ my lord:
and all my ǀ good deǀpends on ǀ you.

3 As for those who are held ǀ holy · on the ǀ earth:
the other ǀ gods · in whom ǀ men deǀlight,

4 Though the idols are many that ǀ men run ǀ after:
their offerings of blood I will not offer
nor take their ǀ name upǀon my ǀ lips.

5 The Lord is my appointed portion ǀ and my ǀ cup:
you ǀ hold my ǀ lot · in your ǀ hands.

6 The share that has fallen to me is in ǀ pleasant ǀ places:
and a fair ǀ land is ǀ my posǀsession.

7 I will bless the Lord who has ǀ given · me ǀ counsel:
at night also ǀ he · has inǀstructed · my ǀ heart.

8 I have set the Lord ǀ always · beǀfore me:
he is at my right ǀ hand · and I ǀ shall not ǀ fall.

†9 Therefore my heart is glad and my ˡ spirit · reˡjoices:
my flesh ˡ also · shall ˡ rest seˡcure.

10 For you will not give me over to the ˡ power of ˡ death:
nor suffer your ˡ faithful one · to ˡ see the ˡ Pit.

11 You will show me the ˡ path of ˡ life:
in your presence is the fulness of joy
and from your right hand flow deˡlights for ˡ everˡ-more.

17

1 Hear my just cause O Lord give ˡ heed to · my ˡ cry:
listen to my prayer that ˡ comes from · no ˡ lying ˡ lips.

2 Let judgement for me come ˡ forth from · your ˡ presence:
and let your ˡ eyes disˡcern the ˡ right.

3 Though you search my heart and visit me ˡ in the ˡ night-time:
though you try me by fire you will ˡ find no ˡ wicked·ness ˡ in me.

4 My mouth does not transgress like the ˡ mouth of ˡ others:
for I have ˡ kept the ˡ word of · your ˡ lips.

†5 My steps have held firm in the way of ˡ your comˡ-mands:
and my feet have not ˡ stumbled ˡ from your ˡ paths.

6 I call upon you O God for you will ˡ surely ˡ answer:
incline your ear to ˡ me and ˡ hear my ˡ words.

7 Show me the wonders of your steadfast love
O saviour of those who come to ˡ you for ˡ refuge:
who by your right hand deliver them‿
from ˡ those that · rise ˡ up aˡgainst them.

8 Keep me as the ˡ apple · of your ˡ eye:
hide me under the ˡ shadow ˡ of your ˡ wings,

9 From the onslaught ˡ of the ˡ wicked:
from my enemies that enˡcircle me · to ˡ take my ˡ life.

10 They have closed their ˡ hearts to ˡ pity:
and their ˡ mouths speak ˡ proud ˡ things.

11 They advance upon me * they surround me on ˡ every ˡ side:
watching how they may ˡ bring me ˡ to the ˡ ground,

†12 Like a lion that is ˡ greedy · for its ˡ prey:
like a lion's whelp ˡ lurking · in ˡ hidden ˡ places.

13 Arise O Lord * stand in their way and ˡ cast them ˡ down:
deliver me from the ˡ wicked ˡ by your ˡ sword.

[14 Slay them by your hand O Lord
slay them so that they ˡ perish · from the ˡ earth:
deˡstroy them · from aˡmong the ˡ living.]

15 But as for your cherished ones
let their bellies be filled and let their ˡ sons be ˡ satisfied:
let them pass on their ˡ wealth ˡ to their ˡ children.

(†)16 And I also shall see your face because my ˈ cause is ˈ just:
when I awake and see you as you ˈ are I ˈ shall be ˈ satisfied.

18

1 I love you O ˈ Lord my ˈ strength:
O Lord my crag my ˈ fortress · and ˈ my deˈliverer,

2 My God the rock to which I ˈ come for ˈ refuge:
my shield my mighty saviour ˈ and my ˈ high deˈfence.

†3 I called to the Lord with ˈ loud · lamenˈtation:
and I was ˈ rescued ˈ from my ˈ enemies.

4 The waves of ˈ death enˈcompassed me:
and the floods of ˈ chaos ˈ overˈwhelmed me;

5 The cords of the grave ˈ tightened · aˈbout me:
and the snares of ˈ death lay ˈ in my ˈ path.

6 In my anguish I ˈ called · to the ˈ Lord:
I cried for ˈ help ˈ to my ˈ God.

7 From his temple he ˈ heard my ˈ voice:
and my cry came ˈ even ˈ to his ˈ ears.

8 The earth heaved and quaked
the foundations of the ˈ hills were ˈ shaken:
they ˈ trembled · beˈcause · he was ˈ angry.

9 Smoke went ǀ out · from his ǀ nostrils:
and a consuming ǀ fire ǀ from his ǀ mouth.

10 He parted the heavens and ǀ came ǀ down:
and there was ǀ darkness ǀ under · his ǀ feet.

11 He rode upon the ǀ cherubim · and ǀ flew:
he came swooping upǀon the ǀ wings · of the ǀ wind.

12 He made the ǀ darkness · his ǀ covering:
and his canopy was thick ǀ cloud and ǀ water·y ǀ darkness.

13 Out of his clouds from the ǀ brightness · beǀfore him:
broke ǀ hailstones · and ǀ coals of ǀ fire.

14 The Lord ǀ thundered · in the ǀ heavens:
the Most ǀ High ǀ uttered · his ǀ voice.

15 He let loose his arrows he scattered them on ǀ every ǀ side:
he hurled down ǀ lightnings · with the ǀ roar · of the ǀ thunderbolt.

16 The springs of the ǀ sea · were unǀcovered:
and the foundǀations · of the ǀ world laid ǀ bare,

17 At your reǀbuke O ǀ Lord:
at the blast of the ǀ breath of ǀ your disǀpleasure.

18 He reached down from on ǀ high and ǀ took me:
he drew me ǀ out of · the ǀ great ǀ waters.

19 He delivered me from my ǀ strongest ǀ enemy:
from my ǀ foes · that were ǀ mightier · than ǀ I.

20 They confronted me in the ǀ day of · my calǀamity:
but the ǀ Lord was ǀ my upǀholder.

21 He brought me out into a ˈ place of ˈ liberty:
and rescued me beˈcause · I deˈlighted · his ˈ heart.

22 The Lord rewarded me for my ˈ righteous ˈ dealing:
he recompensed me according to the ˈ cleanness ˈ of my ˈ hands,

23 Because I had kept to the ˈ ways · of the ˈ Lord:
and had not turned from my ˈ God to ˈ do ˈ evil.

24 For I had an eye to ˈ all his ˈ laws:
and did not ˈ put · his comˈmandments ˈ from me.

25 I was also ˈ blameless · beˈfore him:
and I kept myˈself from ˈ wrongˈdoing.

†26 Therefore the Lord reˈwarded · my ˈ innocence:
because my hands were ˈ undeˈfiled · in his ˈ sight.

27 With the faithful you ˈ show your·self ˈ faithful:
with the ˈ blameless · you ˈ show your·self ˈ blameless;

28 With the ˈ pure · you are ˈ pure:
but with the ˈ crookèd · you ˈ show yourself · perˈverse.

29 For you will save a ˈ humble ˈ people:
but you bring down the ˈ high looks ˈ of the ˈ proud.

30 You light my lamp O ˈ Lord my ˈ God:
you make my ˈ darkness ˈ to be ˈ bright.

†31 For with your help I can charge a ˈ troop of ˈ men:
with the help of my God I can ˈ leap a ˈ city ˈ wall.

32 The way of our God is perfect
the word of the Lord has been ˈ tried · in the ˈ fire:
he is a shield to ˈ all that ˈ trust in ˈ him.

33 For who is | God · but the | Lord:
or who is our | rock | but our | God?

34 It is God that | girded me · with | strength:
that | made my | way | perfect.

35 He made my feet like the | feet · of a | hind:
and set me sure|footed · up|on the | mountains.

36 He taught my | hands to | fight:
and my arms to | aim an | arrow · of | bronze.

37 You gave me the shield of | your sal|vation:
your right hand upheld me
and your swift re|sponse has | made me | great.

38 You lengthened my | stride be|neath me:
and my | ankles | did not | slip.

39 I pursued my enemies and | over|took them:
nor did I turn again | till · I had | made an | end of
them.

40 I smote them till they could | rise no | more:
and they | fell be|neath my | feet.

41 You girded me with | strength · for the | battle:
you threw | down my | adver·saries | under me.

42 You caused my enemies to | show their | backs:
and I de|stroyed | those that | hated me.

43 They cried for help but there was | none to | save
them:
they cried to the | Lord · but he | would not | answer.

44 I pounded them fine as dust be|fore the | wind:
I trod them under | like the | mire · of the | streets.

45 You delivered me from the strife of the peoples
you made me the ǀ head · of the ǀ nations:
a people that I had not ǀ known beǀcame my ǀ servants.

46 As soon as they heard me ǀ they oǀbeyed me:
and aliens ǀ humbled · themǀselves beǀfore me.

47 The strength of the aliens ǀ withered · aǀway:
they came ǀ falter·ing ǀ from their ǀ strongholds.

48 The Lord lives and blessèd ǀ be my ǀ rock:
exalted be the ǀ God of ǀ my salǀvation,

49 The God who sees to it that ǀ I am · aǀvenged:
who subǀdues the ǀ peoples ǀ under me.

50 You set me free from my enemies
you put me out of ǀ reach of · my atǀtackers:
you deǀlivered me · from ǀ vio·lent ǀ men.

51 For this will I give you thanks among the ǀ nations ·
O ǀ Lord:
and sing ǀ praises ǀ to your ǀ name,

†52 To him that gives great triumphs ǀ to his ǀ king:
that deals so faithfully with his anointed
with David and ǀ with his ǀ seed for ǀ ever.

19

1 The heavens declare the | glory · of | God:
and the | firmament · pro|claims his | handiwork;

2 One day | tells it · to an|other:
and night to | night com|muni·cates | knowledge.

3 There is no | speech or | language:
nor | are their | voices | heard;

4 Yet their sound has gone out through | all the | world:
and their | words · to the | ends · of the | earth.

5 There he has pitched a | tent · for the | sun:
which comes out as a bridegroom from his chamber
and rejoices like a | strong · man to | run his |
course.

6 Its rising is at one end of the heavens
and its circuit to their | farthest | bound:
and nothing is | hidden | from its | heat.

7 The law of the Lord is perfect re|viving · the | soul:
the command of the Lord is true |‿
and makes | wise the | simple.

8 The precepts of the Lord are right‿
and re|joice the | heart:
the commandment of the Lord is pure |‿
and gives | light · to the | eyes.

9 The fear of the Lord is clean and en|dures for | ever:
the judgements of the Lord are unchanging‿
and | righteous | every | one.

10 More to be desired are they than gold
even | much fine | gold:
sweeter also than honey
than the | honey · that | drips · from the | comb.

11 Moreover by them is your | servant | taught:
and in keeping them | there is | great re|ward.

12 Who can know his own un|witting | sins?:
O cleanse me | from my | secret | faults.

13 Keep your servant also from presumptuous sins
lest they get the | master·y | over me:
so I shall be clean and | innocent · of | great of|fence.

14 May the words of my mouth and the meditation of my heart
be acceptable | in your | sight:
O Lord my | strength and | my re|deemer.

20

1 May the Lord hear you in the | day of | trouble:
the God of Jacob | lift you | up to | safety.

2 May he send you his | help · from the | sanctuary:
and be your | strong sup|port from | Zion.

3 May he remember | all your | offerings:
and accept with | favour · your | burnt | sacrifices,

4 Grant you your | heart's de|sire:
and ful|fil | all your | purposes.

†5 May we also rejoice in your victory
and triumph in the | name of · our | God:
the Lord per|form all | your pe|titions.

6 Now I know that the Lord will | save · his a|nointed:
that he will answer him from his holy heaven
with the victorious | strength · of his | right | hand.

7 Some put their trust in chariots and | some in | horses:
but we will trust in the | name · of the | Lord our | God.

8 They are brought | down and | fallen:
but we are made | strong and | stand | upright.

9 O Lord | save the | king:
and hear us | when we | call up|on you.

21

1 The king shall rejoice in your | strength O | Lord:
he shall ex|ult in | your sal|vation.

2 You have given him his | heart's de|sire:
you have not de|nied him · the re|quest · of his | lips.

3 For you came to meet him with the | blessings · of suc|cess:
and placed a crown of | gold up|on his | head.

4 He asked you for | life · and you | gave it him:
length of | days for | ever · and | ever.

5 Great is his glory because of | your sal|vation:
you have | clothed him · with | honour · and | majesty.

6 You have given him ever¦lasting · fe¦licity:
and made him ¦ glad · with the ¦ joy of · your ¦ presence.

†7 For the king puts his ¦ trust · in the ¦ Lord:
and through the tender mercy of the Most High ¦‿
he shall ¦ never · be ¦ moved.

8 Your hand shall light up¦on your ¦ enemies:
and your right hand shall ¦ find out ¦ all who ¦ hate you.

9 You will make them like a blazing furnace‿
in the ¦ day of · your ¦ coming:
the Lord will overwhelm them in his wrath‿
and ¦ fire ¦ shall con¦sume them.

10 You will root out their offspring ¦ from the ¦ earth:
and their seed from a¦mong the ¦ children · of ¦ men;

11 Because they have stirred up ¦ evil · a¦gainst you:
and plotted mischief ¦ which they ¦ cannot · per¦-form.

12 Therefore will you set your ¦ shoulder · to¦ward them:
and draw the string of the ¦ bow to ¦ strike at · their ¦ faces.

13 Arise O Lord in your ¦ great ¦ strength:
and we will ¦ sing and ¦ praise your ¦ power.

22

1 My God my God why have ǀ you for|saken me:
why are you so far from helping me
and from the ǀ words ǀ of my ǀ groaning?

2 My God I cry to you by day but you ǀ do not ǀ answer:
and by night ǀ also · I ǀ take no ǀ rest.

3 But you con|tinue ǀ holy:
you that ǀ are the ǀ praise of ǀ Israel.

4 In you our ǀ fathers ǀ trusted:
they ǀ trusted · and ǀ you de|livered them;

5 To you they cried and ǀ they were ǀ saved:
they put their trust in you ǀ and were ǀ not con|-
founded.

6 But as for me I am a worm and ǀ no ǀ man:
the scorn of ǀ men · and de|spised · by the ǀ people.

7 All those that see me ǀ laugh me · to ǀ scorn:
they shoot out their lips at me and ǀ wag their ǀ heads ǀ
saying,

8 'He trusted in the Lord ǀ let him · de|liver him:
let him de|liver him · if ǀ he de|lights in him.'

9 But you are he that took me ǀ out of · the ǀ womb:
that brought me to lie at ǀ peace · on my ǀ mother's ǀ
breast.

10 On you have I been cast ǀ since my ǀ birth:
you are my God ǀ even · from my ǀ mother's ǀ womb.

11 O go not from me for trouble is ǀ hard at ǀ hand:
and ǀ there is ǀ none to ǀ help.

12 Many ǀ oxen · surǀround me:
fat bulls of Bashan close me ǀ in on ǀ every ǀ side.

13 They gape ǀ wide their ǀ mouths at me:
like ǀ lions · that ǀ roar and ǀ rend.

14 I am poured out like water
and all my bones are ǀ out of ǀ joint:
my heart within my ǀ breast · is like ǀ melting ǀ wax.

15 My mouth is dried ǀ up · like a ǀ potsherd:
and my ǀ tongue ǀ clings · to my ǀ gums.

16 My hands and my ǀ feet are ǀ withered:
and you ǀ lay me · in the ǀ dust of ǀ death.

17 For many dogs are ǀ come aǀbout me:
and a band of evilǀdoers ǀ hem me ǀ in.

18 I can count ǀ all my ǀ bones:
they stand ǀ staring · and ǀ gazing · upǀon me.

19 They part my ǀ garments · aǀmong them:
and cast ǀ lots ǀ for my ǀ clothing.

20 O Lord do not ǀ stand far ǀ off:
you are my helper ǀ hasten ǀ to my ǀ aid.

21 Deliver my ǀ body · from the ǀ sword:
my ǀ life · from the ǀ power · of the ǀ dogs;

22 O save me from the ǀ lion's ǀ mouth:
and my afflicted soul from the ǀ horns · of the ǀ wild ǀ oxen.

23 I will tell of your ǀ name · to my ǀ brethren:
in the midst of the congreǀgation ǀ will I ǀ praise you.

24 O praise the Lord all ǀ you that ǀ fear him:
hold him in honour O seed of Jacob
and let the seed of ǀ Israel ǀ stand in ǀ awe of him.

†25 For he has not despised nor abhorred‿
the poor man ǀ in his ǀ misery:
nor did he hide his face from him
but ǀ heard him ǀ when he ǀ cried.

26 From you springs my praise in the ǀ great · congreǀ-gation:
I will pay my vows in the ǀ sight of ǀ all that ǀ fear you;

27 The meek shall eat of the sacrifice ǀ and be ǀ satisfied:
and those who seek the Lord shall praise him
may their ǀ hearts reǀjoice for ǀ ever!

28 Let all the ends of the earth remember‿
and ǀ turn · to the ǀ Lord:
and let all the families of the ǀ nations ǀ worship · be-ǀfore him.

29 For the kingdom ǀ is the ǀ Lord's:
and he shall be ǀ ruler ǀ over · the ǀ nations.

30 How can those who sleep in the earth ǀ do him ǀ homage:
or those that descend to the ǀ dust bow ǀ down beǀfore him?

31 But he has saved my ǀ life · for himǀself:
and ǀ my posǀterity · shall ǀ serve him.

†32 This shall be told of my Lord to a future ǀ generǀation:
and his righteousness declared‿
to a people yet unǀborn that ǀ he has ǀ done it.

23

1 The Lord | is my | shepherd:
therefore | can I | lack | nothing.

2 He will make me lie down in | green | pastures:
and | lead me · be|side still | waters.

3 He will re|fresh my | soul:
and guide me in right pathways | for his | name's |
sake.

4 Though I walk through the valley of the shadow of‿
death I will | fear no | evil:
for you are with me
your | rod · and your | staff | comfort me.

5 You spread a table before me
in the face of | those who | trouble me:
you have anointed my head with oil | and my | cup ·
will be | full.

6 Surely your goodness and loving-kindness‿
will follow me * all the | days · of my | life:
and I shall dwell in the | house · of the | Lord for |
ever.

24

1 The earth is the Lord's and | all · that is | in it:
the compass of the | world and | those who | dwell therein.

2 For he has founded it up|on the | seas:
and es|tablished it · up|on the | waters.

3 Who shall ascend the | hill · of the | Lord:
or who shall | stand · in his | holy | place?

4 He that has clean hands and a | pure | heart:
who has not set his soul upon idols
nor | sworn his | oath · to a | lie.

5 He shall receive | blessing · from the | Lord:
and recompense from the | God of | his sal|vation.

6 Of such a kind as this are | those who | seek him:
those who seek your | face O | God of | Jacob.

7 Lift up your heads O you gates
and be lifted up you ever|lasting | doors:
and the King of | glory | shall come | in.

8 Who is the | King of | glory?:
the Lord strong and mighty * the | Lord | mighty · in | battle.

9 Lift up your heads O you gates
and be lifted up you ever|lasting | doors:
and the King of | glory | shall come | in.

10 Who is the | King of | glory?:
the Lord of hosts | he · is the | King of | glory.

25

1 In you O Lord my God have I ꞁ put my ꞁ hope:
in you have I trusted let me not be ashamed
nor let my ꞁ ene·mies ꞁ triumph ꞁ over me.

2 Let none who wait for you be ꞁ put to ꞁ shame:
but let those that break faith‿
be conꞁfounded · and ꞁ gain ꞁ nothing.

3 Show me your ꞁ ways O ꞁ Lord:
and ꞁ teach me ꞁ your ꞁ paths.

4 Lead me in the ways of your ꞁ truth and ꞁ teach me:
for you are the ꞁ God of ꞁ my salꞁvation.

5 In you have I hoped ꞁ all the · day ꞁ long:
beꞁcause of · your ꞁ goodness · O ꞁ Lord.

6 Call to mind your compassion and your ꞁ loving-ꞁ kindness:
for ꞁ they are ꞁ from of ꞁ old.

7 Remember not the sins of my youth nor ꞁ my transꞁ-gressions:
but according ꞁ to your ꞁ mercy ꞁ think on me.

8 Good and upright ꞁ is the ꞁ Lord:
therefore will he direct ꞁ sinners ꞁ in the ꞁ way.

†9 The meek he will guide in the ꞁ path of ꞁ justice:
and ꞁ teach the ꞁ humble · his ꞁ ways.

10 All the paths of the Lord are ꞁ faithful · and ꞁ true:
for those who keep his ꞁ covenant · and ꞁ his comꞁ-mandments.

11 For your name's ¦ sake O ¦ Lord:
be merciful to my ¦ sin though ¦ it is ¦ great.

12 Who is he that ¦ fears the ¦ Lord?:
him will the Lord direct in the ¦ way that ¦ he should ¦ choose.

13 His soul shall ¦ dwell at ¦ ease:
and his ¦ children · shall in¦herit · the ¦ land.

14 The confidences of God belong to ¦ those that ¦ fear him:
and his covenant shall ¦ give them ¦ under¦standing.

15 My eyes are ever ¦ looking · to the ¦ Lord:
for he will bring my ¦ feet ¦ out of · the ¦ net.

16 Turn your face toward me ¦ and be ¦ gracious:
for ¦ I am · a¦lone · and in ¦ misery.

17 O free my ¦ heart from ¦ pain:
and bring me ¦ out of ¦ my dis¦tress.

18 Give heed to my af¦fliction · and ad¦versity:
and for¦give me ¦ all my ¦ sins.

19 Consider my enemies how ¦ many · they ¦ are:
and they bear a ¦ vio·lent ¦ hate a¦gainst me.

20 O keep my ¦ life · and de¦liver me:
put me not to shame for I ¦ come to ¦ you for ¦ refuge.

21 Let innocence and integrity ¦ be my ¦ guard:
for in ¦ you ¦ have I ¦ hoped.

†22 O God de¦liver ¦ Israel:
out of ¦ all his ¦ tribu¦lation.

26

1 Give judgement for me O Lord
for I have walked in ǀ my inǀtegrity:
I have trusted in the ǀ Lord and ǀ not ǀ wavered.

2 Put me to the test O ǀ Lord and ǀ prove me:
try my ǀ mind ǀ and my ǀ heart.

3 For your steadfast love has been ever beǀfore my ǀ eyes:
and ǀ I have ǀ walked in · your ǀ truth.

4 I have not ǀ sat · with deǀceivers:
nor conǀsorted ǀ with the ǀ hypocrites;

5 I hate the asǀsembly · of the ǀ wicked:
I will not ǀ sit ǀ with the · unǀgodly.

6 I wash my hands in ǀ innocence · O ǀ Lord:
that I may ǀ go aǀbout your ǀ altar,

†7 And lift up the ǀ voice of ǀ thanksgiving:
to tell of ǀ all your ǀ marvel·lous ǀ works.

8 Lord I love the house of your ǀ habitǀation:
and the ǀ place · where your ǀ glory ǀ dwells

9 Do not sweep me aǀway with ǀ sinners:
nor my ǀ life with ǀ men of ǀ blood,

10 In whose hand is aǀbominǀation:
and their right ǀ hand is ǀ full of ǀ bribes.

11 As for me I walk in ǀ my inǀtegrity:
O ransom me ǀ and be ǀ favourable · toǀward me.

†12 My foot stands on an ǀ even ǀ path:
I will bless the ǀ Lord · in the ǀ great · congreǀgation.

27

1 The Lord is my light and my salvation
whom then ¦ shall I ¦ fear?:
the Lord is the stronghold of my life
of whom ¦ shall I ¦ be a¦fraid?

2 When the wicked even my enemies and my foes
come upon me ¦ to de¦vour me:
they shall ¦ stumble ¦ and ¦ fall.

3 If an army encamp against me
my heart shall ¦ not · be a¦fraid:
and if war should rise a¦gainst me ¦ yet · will I ¦ trust.

4 One thing I have asked from the Lord which I ¦ will
re¦quire:
that I may dwell in the house of the Lord ¦‿
all the ¦ days · of my ¦ life,

†5 To see the fair ¦ beauty · of the ¦ Lord:
and to ¦ seek his ¦ will · in his ¦ temple.

6 For he will hide me under his shelter in the ¦ day of ¦
trouble:
and conceal me in the shadow of his tent
and set me ¦ high up¦on a ¦ rock.

7 And now he will lift ¦ up my ¦ head:
above my ¦ ene·mies ¦ round a¦bout me.

†8 And I will offer sacrifices in his sanctuary‿
with ¦ exul¦tation:
I will sing I will sing ¦ praises ¦ to the ¦ Lord.

9 O Lord hear my ¦ voice · when I ¦ cry:
have ¦ mercy · up¦on me · and ¦ answer me.

10 My heart has said of you ǀ 'Seek his ǀ face':
your ǀ face Lord ǀ I will ǀ seek.

11 Do not ǀ hide your ǀ face from me:
or thrust your ǀ servant · aǀside · in disǀpleasure;

12 For you have ǀ been my ǀ helper:
do not cast me away or forsake me O ǀ God of ǀ my salǀvation.

†13 Though my father and my ǀ mother · forǀsake me:
the ǀ Lord will ǀ take me ǀ up.

14 Teach me your ǀ way O ǀ Lord:
and lead me in an even path ǀ for they ǀ lie in ǀ wait for me.

15 Do not give me over to the ǀ will of · my ǀ enemies:
for false witnesses have risen against me
and ǀ those who ǀ breathe out ǀ violence.

16 But I believe that I shall surely see the ǀ goodness · of‿the ǀ Lord:
in the ǀ land ǀ of the ǀ living.

17 O wait for the Lord
stand firm and he will ǀ strengthen · your ǀ heart:
and ǀ wait I ǀ say · for the ǀ Lord.

28

1 To you will I cry O Lord my Rock
be not | deaf · to my | prayer:
lest if you turn away silent
I become like those that go | down | to the | grave.

2 Hear the voice of my supplication
when I cry to | you for | help:
when I lift up my hands‿
towards the | holi·est | place of · your | sanctuary.

3 Do not snatch me away with the ungodly
with the | evil|doers:
who speak peace to their neighbours
but nourish | malice | in their | hearts.

4 Repay them ac|cording · to their | deeds:
and according to the | wickedness · of | their en|-deavours;

5 Requite them for the | work · of their | hands:
and | give them | their de|serts.

6 For they pay no heed to the Lord's acts
nor to the operation | of his | hands:
therefore shall he break them | down · and not | build them | up.

7 Let the Lord's | name be | praised:
for he has heard the | voice · of my | suppli|cation.

8 The Lord is my strength and my shield
in him my heart trusts and | I am | helped:
therefore my heart dances for joy
and in my | song | will I | praise him.

9 The Lord is the ǀ strength · of his ǀ people:
and a sure refuge for ǀ his anǀointed ǀ king.

10 O save your people * and give your ǀ blessing · to your ǀ own:
be their shepherd and ǀ bear them ǀ up for ǀ ever.

29

1 Ascribe to the Lord you ǀ sons of ǀ heaven:
ascribe to the ǀ Lord ǀ glory · and ǀ might.

2 Ascribe to the Lord the honour ǀ due · to his ǀ name:
O worship the Lord in the ǀ beauty ǀ of his ǀ holiness.

3 The voice of the Lord is upǀon the ǀ waters:
the God of glory thunders the Lord upǀon the ǀ great ǀ waters.

4 The voice of the Lord is mighty in ǀ operǀation:
the voice of the ǀ Lord · is a ǀ glori·ous ǀ voice.

5 The voice of the Lord ǀ breaks the ǀ cedar-trees:
the Lord breaks in ǀ pieces · the ǀ cedars · of ǀ Lebanon.

6 He makes them ǀ skip · like a ǀ calf:
Lebanon and Sirion ǀ like a ǀ young wild ǀ ox.

7 The voice of the Lord diǀvides the ǀ lightning-flash:
the voice of the Lord whirls the sands of the desert
the Lord ǀ whirls the ǀ desert · of ǀ Kadesh.

8 The voice of the Lord rends the terebinth trees
and strips ǀ bare the ǀ forests:
in his ǀ temple ǀ all cry ǀ 'Glory'.

9 The Lord sits enthroned a|bove the | water-flood:
the Lord sits en|throned · as a | king for | ever.

10 The Lord will give | strength · to his | people:
the Lord will give to his | people · the | blessing · of | peace.

30

1 I will exalt you O Lord
for you have drawn me | up · from the | depths:
and have not suffered my | foes to | triumph | over me.

2 O Lord my | God I | cried to you:
and | you have | made me | whole.

†3 You brought me back O Lord from the | land of | silence:
you saved my life‿
from among | those that · go | down · to the | Pit.

4 Sing praises to the Lord all | you his | faithful ones:
and give | thanks · to his | holy | name.

5 For if in his anger is havoc
in his good | favour · is | life:
heaviness may endure for a night
but | joy comes | in the | morning.

6 In my prosperity I said 'I shall | never · be | moved:
your goodness O Lord has | set me · on so | firm a | hill.'

7 Then you | hid your | face from me:
and | I was | greatly · dis|mayed.

8 I cried to ǀ you O ǀ God:
and made my petition ǀ humbly ǀ to my ǀ Lord.

9 'What profit is there in my blood
if I go ǀ down · to the ǀ Pit:
can the dust give you thanks ǀ ‿
or deǀclare your ǀ faithfulness?

†10 'Hear O ǀ Lord · and be ǀ merciful:
O ǀ Lord ǀ be my ǀ helper.'

11 You have turned my lamentation ǀ into ǀ dancing:
you have put off my sackcloth and ǀ girded ǀ me with ǀ joy,

12 That my heart may sing your praise and ǀ never · be ǀ silent:
O Lord my God I will ǀ give you ǀ thanks for ǀ ever.

31

1 To you Lord have I ǀ come for ǀ shelter:
let me ǀ never · be ǀ put to ǀ shame.

2 O deliver me ǀ in your ǀ righteousness:
incline your ear to me ǀ and be ǀ swift to ǀ save me.

3 Be for me a rock of refuge a fortress ǀ to deǀfend me:
for you are my ǀ high rock ǀ and my ǀ stronghold.

4 Lead me and guide me for your ǀ name's ǀ sake:
bring me out of the net that they have secretly laid for me * for ǀ you ǀ are my ǀ strength.

5 Into your hands I com|mit my | spirit:
you will redeem me | O Lord | God of | truth.

6 I hate those that | clutch vain | idols:
but my | trust is | in the | Lord.

7 I will rejoice and be glad in your | loving-|kindness:
for you have looked on my distress
and | known me | in ad|versity.

8 You have not given me over to the | power · of the | enemy:
you have set my feet where | I may | walk at | liberty.

9 Have mercy upon me O Lord for | I am · in | trouble:
my eye wastes away for grief
my throat also | and my | inward | parts.

10 For my life wears out in sorrow‿
and my | years with | sighing:
my strength fails me in my affliction
and my | bones | are con|sumed.

11 I am become the scorn of | all my | enemies:
and my neighbours | wag their | heads · in de|rision.

12 I am a thing of | horror · to my | friends:
and those that see me in the | street | shrink | from me.

13 I am forgotten like a dead man | out of | mind:
I have be|come · like a | broken | vessel.

14 For I hear the | whispering · of | many:
and | fear · is on | every | side;

15 While they plot to|gether · a|gainst me:
and scheme to | take a|way my | life.

16 But in you Lord have I ǀ put my ǀ trust:
I have said ǀ 'You ǀ are my ǀ God.'

17 All my days are ǀ in your ǀ hand:
O deliver me from the power of my ǀ enemies · ‿
and ǀ from my ǀ persecutors.

18 Make your face to shine upǀon your ǀ servant:
and save me ǀ for your ǀ mercy's ǀ sake.

19 O Lord let me not be confounded
for I have ǀ called upǀon you:
but let the wicked be put to shame
and brought to ǀ silence ǀ in the ǀ grave.

20 Let the lying ǀ lips be ǀ dumb:
that in pride and contempt‿
speak such ǀ insolence · aǀgainst the ǀ just.

21 O how plentiful is your goodness
stored up for ǀ those that ǀ fear you:
and prepared in the sight of men
for all who ǀ come to ǀ you for ǀ refuge.

22 You will hide them in the cover of your presence‿
from the ǀ plots of ǀ men:
you will shelter them in your refuge ǀ‿
from the ǀ strife of ǀ tongues.

23 Blessèd be the ǀ Lord our ǀ God:
for he has wonderfully shown me his steadfast love
when I was ǀ as a ǀ city · beǀsieged.

24 When I was afraid I ǀ said in · my ǀ haste:
'I am ǀ cut off ǀ from your ǀ sight.'

25 But you heard the voice of my ǀ supplicǀation:
when I ǀ cried to ǀ you for ǀ help.

26 Love the Lord all ˡ you his ˡ faithful ones:
for the Lord guards the true
but ˡ fully · reˡquites the ˡ proud.

†27 Be strong and let your ˡ heart take ˡ courage:
all ˡ you that ˡ hope · in the ˡ Lord.

32

1 Blessèd is he whose ˡ sin · is forˡgiven:
whose inˡiquity · is ˡ put aˡway.

2 Blessèd is the man to whom the Lord imˡputes no ˡ blame:
and in whose ˡ spirit · there ˡ is no ˡ guile.

3 For whilst I ˡ held my ˡ tongue:
my bones wasted aˡway · with my ˡ daily · comˡplaining.

4 Your hand was heavy upon me ˡ day and ˡ night:
and my moisture was dried ˡ up · like a ˡ drought in ˡ summer.

5 Then I ackˡnowledged · my ˡ sin to you:
and my inˡiquity · I ˡ did not ˡ hide;

6 I said 'I will confess my transˡgressions · to the ˡ Lord':
and so you forgave the ˡ wicked·ness ˡ of my ˡ sin.

7 For this cause shall everyone that is faithful‿
make his prayer to you * in the ˡ day of ˡ trouble:
and in the time of the great water-floods ˡ‿
they shall ˡ not come ˡ near him.

8 You are a place to hide me in
you will pre|serve me · from | trouble:
you will surround me with de|liverance · on | every | side.

9 'I will instruct you
and direct you in the way that | you should | go:
I will fasten my eye up|on you · and | give you | counsel.

10 'Be not like horse or mule that have no | under|standing:
whose forward course must be | curbed with | bit and | bridle.'

11 Great tribulations remain | for the · un|godly:
but whoever puts his trust in the Lord
mercy em|braces him · on | every | side.

12 Rejoice in the Lord you righteous | and be | glad:
and shout for joy all | you · that are | true of | heart.

33

1 Rejoice in the | Lord you | righteous:
for it be|fits the | just to | praise him.

2 Give the Lord thanks up|on the | harp:
and sing his praise to the | lute of | ten | strings.

3 O sing him a | new | song:
make sweetest | melody · with | shouts of | praise.

4 For the word of the | Lord is | true:
and | all his | works are | faithful.

5 He loves | righteousness · and | justice:
the earth is filled with the loving-|kindness | of the |
Lord.

6 By the word of the Lord were the | heavens | made:
and their numberless | stars · by the | breath of · his |
mouth.

7 He gathered the waters of the sea as | in a | water-skin:
and laid up the | deep | in his | treasuries.

8 Let the whole earth | fear the | Lord:
and let all the inhabitants of the | world | stand in |
awe of him.

9 For he spoke and | it was | done:
he commanded | and it | stood | fast.

10 The Lord frustrates the | counsels · of the | nations:
he brings to nothing the de|vices | of the | peoples.

11 But the counsels of the Lord shall en|dure for | ever:
the purposes of his heart from gener|ation · to |
gener|ation.

12 Blessèd is that nation whose | God · is the | Lord:
the people he chose to | be his | own pos|session.

13 The Lord looks down from heaven
and surveys all the | children · of | men:
he considers from his dwelling-place‿
all the in|habit·ants | of the | earth;

14 He who fashioned the | hearts of · them | all:
and compre|hends all | that they | do.

15 A king is not saved by a | mighty | army:
nor is a warrior de|livered · by | much | strength;

16 A horse is a vain hope to | save a | man:
nor can he rescue | any · by his | great | power.

17 But the eye of the Lord is on | those that | fear him:
on those that trust in | his un|failing | love,

18 To de|liver them · from | death:
and to | feed them · in the | time of | dearth.

19 We have waited eagerly | for the | Lord:
for | he is · our | help · and our | shield.

20 Surely our hearts shall re|joice in | him:
for we have | trusted · in his | holy | name.

†21 Let your merciful kindness be up|on us · O | Lord:
even as our | hope | is in | you.

34

1 I will bless the | Lord con|tinually:
his praise shall be | always | in my | mouth.

2 Let my soul | boast · of the | Lord:
the humble shall | hear it | and re|joice.

3 O praise the | Lord with | me:
let us ex|alt his | name to|gether.

4 For I sought the Lord's | help · and he | answered:
and he | freed me · from | all my | fears.

5 Look towards him and be | bright with | joy:
your | faces · shall | not · be a|shamed.

6 Here is a wretch who cried and the | Lord | heard him:
and | saved him · from | all his | troubles.

7 The angel of the Lord encamps round | those who | fear him:
and de|livers · them | in their | need.

8 O taste and see that the | Lord is | good:
happy the | man who | hides in | him!

9 Fear the Lord all | you his | holy ones:
for those who | fear him | never | lack.

10 Lions may suffer | want · and go | hungry:
but those who seek the | Lord lack | nothing | good.

11 Come my children | listen · to | me:
and I will | teach you · the | fear · of the | Lord.

12 Which of you | relish·es | life:
wants | time · to en|joy good | things?

13 Keep your | tongue from | evil:
and your | lips from | telling | lies.

14 Turn from evil and | do | good:
seek | peace | and pur|sue it.

15 The eyes of God are | on the | righteous:
and his | ears to|wards their | cry.

16 The Lord sets his face against | wrong|doers:
to root out their | memo·ry | from the | earth.

17 The righteous cry the | Lord | hears it:
and | frees them · from | all · their af|flictions.

18 The Lord is close to those who are | broken-|hearted:
and the | crushed in | spirit · he | saves.

19 The trials of the ¦ righteous · are ¦ many:
but our God de¦livers · him ¦ from them ¦ all.

20 He guards ¦ all his ¦ bones:
so ¦ that not ¦ one is ¦ broken.

21 Evil will ¦ slay the ¦ wicked:
and those who hate the ¦ righteous · will ¦ be de¦stroyed.

22 The Lord ransoms the ¦ lives · of his ¦ servants:
and none who hide in ¦ him will ¦ be de¦stroyed.

35

1 Contend O Lord with those who con¦tend with ¦ me:
fight against ¦ those that ¦ fight a¦gainst me.

2 Take up ¦ shield and ¦ buckler:
and a¦rise a¦rise to ¦ help me.

3 Draw the spear
and bar the way against ¦ those · that pur¦sue me:
say to me ¦ 'I am ¦ your de¦liverer.'

4 Let those that seek my life‿
be put to ¦ shame · and dis¦graced:
let those that plot my destruction‿
be ¦ turned ¦ back · and con¦founded.

5 Let them be like chaff be¦fore the ¦ wind:
with the ¦ angel · of the ¦ Lord ¦ driving them;

6 Let their way be ¦ dark and ¦ slippery:
with the ¦ angel · of the ¦ Lord pur¦suing.

7 For without cause‿
they have secretly ˡ spread a ˡ net for me:
without cause they have ˡ dug a ˡ pit · to enˡtrap me.

8 Let sudden disˡaster ˡ strike them:
let the net that they have hidden catch them
let them ˡ fall to ˡ their deˡstruction.

9 Then shall my soul be ˡ joyful · in the ˡ Lord:
and I will reˡjoice in ˡ his deˡliverance.

10 All my bones shall say ˡ 'Lord · who is ˡ like you?:
for you deliver the poor man‿
from him that is too strong for him
the poor and needy‿
from ˡ him that ˡ would deˡspoil them.'

11 Malicious witnesses rise ˡ up aˡgainst me:
I am questioned about things of ˡ which I ˡ know ˡ
nothing.

12 They repay me ˡ evil · for ˡ good:
I am as ˡ one beˡreaved of · his ˡ children.

13 Yet when they were sick I ˡ put on ˡ sackcloth:
I afˡflicted · myˡself with ˡ fasting.

14 And if my prayer returned unanswered ˡ to my ˡ bosom:
I went about mourning
as though for a ˡ brother ˡ or a · comˡpanion;

15 I was bowed ˡ down with ˡ grief:
as ˡ though · for my ˡ own ˡ mother.

16 But when I stumbled they rejoiced and gathered‿
together * they gathered toˡgether · aˡgainst me:
as though they were strangers I never knew
they ˡ tore at · me ˡ without ˡ ceasing.

†17 When I ǀ slipped they ǀ mocked me:
and ǀ gnashed · at me ǀ with their ǀ teeth.

18 Lord how long will ǀ you look ǀ on?:
take me from the evil they intend
take me ǀ from aǀmidst the ǀ lions.

19 And I will give you thanks in the ǀ great · congreǀgation:
I will ǀ praise you · in the ǀ throng · of the ǀ people.

20 Let not those that wrongfully are my enemies ǀ‿
triumph ǀ over me:
let not those that hate me without cause ǀ‿
mock me ǀ with their ǀ eyes.

21 For they speak words that do not ǀ make for ǀ peace:
they invent lies against those that are ǀ quiet ǀ in the ǀ
land.

22 They stretch their mouths to ǀ jeer at me · and ǀ say:
'Aha aha! We have ǀ seen ǀ all that · we ǀ wish!'

23 And you also have seen O Lord ǀ do not · be ǀ silent:
O God ǀ go not ǀ far ǀ from me.

24 Bestir yourself awake to ǀ do me ǀ right:
to plead my ǀ cause O ǀ Lord my ǀ God.

25 Judge me O Lord my God according ǀ to your ǀ
righteousness:
and let them ǀ not reǀjoice ǀ over me.

26 Let them not say in their hearts 'We ǀ have our ǀ wish':
let them not ǀ say 'We ǀ have deǀstroyed him.'

27 Let those that rejoice at my hurt
be disgraced and confounded ǀ altoǀgether:
let those that lord it over me‿
be ǀ clothed in ǀ shame · and disǀhonour.

28 But let those that long for my vindication
shout for | joy · and re|joice:
let them say always that the Lord is great
who takes such de|light · in his | servant's | good.

29 And my tongue shall | speak of · your | righteousness:
and of your | praise | all the · day | long.

36

1 The transgressor speaks‿
from the wickedness in his | own | heart:
there is no fear of | God be|fore his | eyes.

2 For he flatters himself in his | own | sight:
he hates his in|iquity · to be | found | out.

3 The words of his mouth are wickedness | and de|ceit:
he has ceased to act | wisely · and | do | good.

4 He plots mischief as he lies up|on his | bed:
he has set himself on a path that is not good
he | does not | spurn | evil.

5 Your unfailing kindness O Lord is | in the | heavens:
and your faithfulness | reaches | to the | clouds.

6 Your righteousness is like the | strong | mountains:
and your justice as the great deep
you O Lord | save both | man and | beast.

7 How precious O God is your en|during | kindness:
the children of men shall take refuge‿
under the | shadow | of your | wings.

8 They shall be satisfied‿
with the good things | of your | house:
and you will give them drink‿
from the | river · of | your de|lights.

9 For with you is the | well of | life:
and in your | light shall | we see | light.

10 O continue your merciful kindness‿
toward | those who | know you:
and your righteous dealing‿
to | those · that are | true of | heart.

11 Let not the foot of the | proud · come a|gainst me:
nor the hand of the un|godly | drive · me a|way.

12 There are they fallen | those who · do | evil:
they are thrust down and | shall not | rise a|gain.

37

1 Do not | vie · with the | wicked:
or | envy | those that · do | wrong;

2 For they will soon | wither · like the | grass:
and fade a|way · like the | green | leaf.

3 Trust in the | Lord and · do | good:
and you shall dwell in the land‿
and | feed in | safe | pastures.

4 Let the Lord be | your de|light:
and he will | grant you · your | heart's de|sire.

5 Commit your ǀ way · to the ǀ Lord:
trust ǀ him and ǀ he will ǀ act.

6 He will make your righteousness‿
shine as ǀ clear · as the ǀ light:
and your ǀ inno·cence ǀ as the ǀ noonday.

7 Be still before the Lord * and wait ǀ patient·ly ǀ for him:
do not be vexed when a man prospers
when he puts his ǀ evil ǀ purposes · to ǀ work.

8 Let go of anger and aǀbandon ǀ wrath:
let not envy ǀ move you · to ǀ do ǀ evil.

9 For the wicked shall be ǀ cut ǀ down:
but those who wait for the ǀ Lord · shall posǀsess the ǀ land.

10 In a little while the ungodly shall ǀ be no ǀ more:
you will look for him in his place‿
but ǀ he will ǀ not be ǀ found.

†11 But the meek shall posǀsess the ǀ land:
and enǀjoy · the aǀbundance · of ǀ peace.

12 The ungodly man plots aǀgainst the ǀ righteous:
and ǀ gnashes · at him ǀ with his ǀ teeth.

13 But the Lord shall ǀ laugh him · to ǀ scorn:
for he sees that the ǀ day · for his ǀ overthrow · is ǀ near.

14 The ungodly have drawn the sword and ǀ strung the ǀ bow:
to strike down the poor and needy
to slaughter ǀ those that ǀ walk in ǀ innocence.

15 Their swords shall pierce their ǀ own ǀ hearts:
and their ǀ bows ǀ shall be ǀ broken.

16 Though the righteous man | has · but a | little:
it is better than the great | wealth of | the un|godly.

17 For the strong arm of the ungodly | shall be | broken:
but the | Lord up|holds the | righteous.

18 The Lord cares for the | lives · of the | innocent:
and their heritage | shall be | theirs for | ever.

19 They shall not be put to shame in the | evil | days:
but in time of famine | they shall | eat their | fill.

†20 As for the ungodly they shall perish
they are the enemies | of the | Lord:
like fuel in a furnace they shall | vanish · a|way in smoke.

21 The ungodly man borrows but does | not re|pay:
but the | righteous · is | gracious · and | gives.

22 Those who are blessed by God shall pos|sess the | land:
but those whom he has | cursed · shall be | cut | down.

23 If a man's steps are | guided · by the | Lord:
and | he de|lights in · his | way,

24 Though he stumble he shall | not fall | headlong:
for the Lord | holds him | by the | hand.

25 I have been young and | now am | old:
but I never saw the righteous man forsaken
or his | children | begging · their | bread.

26 He is ever | gracious · and | lends:
and his | children | shall be | blessed.

27 Turn from evil and ˡ do ˡ good:
and you shall ˡ dwell · in the ˡ land for ˡ ever.

28 For the ˡ Lord loves ˡ justice:
he will ˡ not forˡsake his ˡ faithful ones.

29 But the unjust shall be deˡstroyed for ˡ ever:
and the children of the unˡgodly · shall be ˡ cut down.

30 The just shall posˡsess the ˡ land:
and they shall ˡ dwell in ˡ it for ˡ ever.

31 The mouth of the righteous man ˡ utters ˡ wisdom:
and his ˡ tongue speaks ˡ what is ˡ right.

32 The law of his God is ˡ in his ˡ heart:
and his ˡ footsteps ˡ will not ˡ slip.

33 The ungodly man watches ˡ out · for the ˡ righteous:
and ˡ seeks ocˡcasion · to ˡ slay him.

34 But the Lord will not abandon him ˡ to his ˡ power:
nor let him be conˡdemned when ˡ he is ˡ judged.

†35 Wait for the Lord and ˡ hold to · his ˡ way:
and he will raise you up to possess the land
to see the unˡgodly · when ˡ they are · deˡstroyed.

36 I have seen the ungodly in ˡ terri·fying ˡ power:
spreading himself ˡ like a · luxˡuri·ant ˡ tree;

37 I passed by again and ˡ he was ˡ gone:
I searched for him ˡ but · he could ˡ not be ˡ found.

38 Observe the blameless man and conˡsider · the ˡ upright:
for the man of ˡ peace shall ˡ have posˡterity.

39 But transgressors shall be deˡstroyed · altoˡgether:
and the posterity of the ˡ wicked · shall be ˡ cut ˡ down.

40 Deliverance for the righteous shall ¦ come · from the ¦ Lord:
he is their ¦ strength in ¦ time of ¦ trouble.

41 The Lord will help them ¦ and de¦liver them:
he will save them from the ungodly and deliver them because they ¦ come to ¦ him for ¦ refuge.

38

1 O Lord rebuke me not ¦ in your ¦ anger:
nor chasten me ¦ in your ¦ fierce dis¦pleasure.

2 For your arrows have been ¦ aimed a¦gainst me:
and your hand has come ¦ down ¦ heavy · up¦on me.

3 There is no health in my flesh because of your ¦ indig¦nation:
nor soundness in my bones by ¦ reason ¦ of my ¦ sin.

4 The tide of my iniquities has gone ¦ over · my ¦ head:
their weight is a burden too ¦ heavy · for ¦ me to ¦ bear.

5 My wounds ¦ stink and ¦ fester:
be¦cause ¦ of my ¦ foolishness.

6 I am bowed down and ¦ brought so ¦ low:
that I go ¦ mourning ¦ all the · day ¦ long.

7 For my loins are filled with a ¦ burning ¦ pain:
and there is no sound ¦ part in ¦ all my ¦ body.

8 I am numbed and ¦ stricken · to the ¦ ground:
I cry aloud in the ¦ yearning ¦ of my ¦ heart.

9 O Lord   all I long for | is be|fore you:
and my deep sighing | is not | hidden | from you.

10 My heart is in tumult   my | strength | fails me:
and even the | light of · my | eyes has | gone from me.

11 My friends and my companions hold aloof from | my af|fliction:
and my | kinsmen | stand far | off.

12 Those who seek my | life | strike at me:
and those that desire my hurt spread evil tales and murmur | slanders | all the | day.

13 But I am like a deaf man and | hear | nothing:
like one that is dumb who | does not | open · his | mouth.

14 So I have become as one who | cannot | hear:
in whose | mouth · there is | no re|tort.

15 For in you Lord have I | put my | trust:
and you will | answer me · O | Lord my | God.

16 For I prayed   'Let them never ex|ult | over me:
those who turn arrogant | when my | foot | slips.'

17 Truly I am | ready · to | fall:
and my | pain is | with me · con|tinually.

18 But I ac|knowledge · my | wickedness:
and I am filled with | sorrow | at my | sin.

19 Those that are my enemies without cause are | great in | number:
and those who hate me | wrongful|ly are | many.

20 Those also who repay evil for good | are a|gainst me:
because I | seek | after | good.

†21 Forsake me not O Lord
go not far | from me · my | God:
hasten to my | help O | Lord · my sal|vation.

39

1 I said 'I will keep watch over my ways
lest I | sin · with my | tongue:
I will keep a guard on my mouth
while the | wicked · are | in my | sight.'

2 I held my tongue and | said | nothing:
I kept | silent · but | found no | comfort.

3 My pain was increased my heart grew | hot with|in me:
while I mused the fire blazed and I | spoke | with my | tongue;

4 'Lord let me | know my | end:
and the | number | of my | days,

†5 'That I may know how | short my | time is:
for you have made my days but a handsbreadth
and my whole | span · is as | nothing · be|fore you.'

6 Surely every man though he stand secure | is but | breath:
man | lives · as a | passing | shadow.

7 The riches he heaps are but a | puff of | wind:
and he cannot | tell | who will | gather them.

8 And now Lord ˡ what is · my ˡ hope?:
truly my ˡ hope ˡ is in ˡ you.

9 O deliver me from ˡ all · my transˡgressions:
do not ˡ make me · the ˡ butt of ˡ fools.

10 I was dumb I did not ˡ open · my ˡ mouth:
for surely ˡ it was ˡ your ˡ doing.

11 Take away your ˡ plague ˡ from me:
I am brought to an ˡ end · by the ˡ blows · of your ˡ hand.

12 When with rebukes you chastise a ˡ man for ˡ sin:
you cause his fair looks to dissolve in putrefaction surely ˡ every · man ˡ is but ˡ breath.

13 Hear my prayer O Lord and give ˡ ear to · my ˡ cry:
be not ˡ silent ˡ at my ˡ tears.

14 For I am but a ˡ stranger · with ˡ you:
a passing guest as ˡ all my ˡ fathers ˡ were.

15 Turn your eye from me that I may ˡ smile aˡgain:
before I go ˡ hence and ˡ am no ˡ more.

40

1 I waited patiently ˡ for the ˡ Lord:
and he inˡclined to me · and ˡ heard my ˡ cry.

2 He brought me up from the pit of roaring waters out of the ˡ mire and ˡ clay:
and set my feet upon a ˡ rock and made ˡ firm my ˡ foothold.

3 And he has put a new ǀ song · in my ǀ mouth:
even a song of ǀ thanks·giving ǀ to our ǀ God.

4 Many shall ǀ see it · and ǀ fear:
and shall ǀ put their ǀ trust · in the ǀ Lord.

5 Blessèd is the man who has made the ǀ Lord his ǀ hope:
who has not turned to the proud
or to those who ǀ wander ǀ in deǀceit.

6 O Lord my God
great are the wonderful things which you have done
and your thoughts which ǀ are toǀwards us:
there is none to ǀ be comǀpared with ǀ you;

†7 Were I to deǀclare them · and ǀ speak of them:
they are more than I am ǀ able ǀ to exǀpress.

8 Sacrifice and offering you do ǀ not deǀsire:
but my ǀ ears · you have ǀ marked · for oǀbedience;

9 Burnt-offering and sin-offering you have ǀ not reǀ-quired:
then ǀ said I ǀ Lo I ǀ come.

10 In the scroll of the book it is written of me
that I should ǀ do your ǀ will:
O my God I long to do it * your ǀ law deǀlights my ǀ heart.

11 I have declared your righteousness‿
in the ǀ great · congreǀgation:
I have not restrained my lips O ǀ Lord‿
and ǀ that you ǀ know.

12 I have not hidden your righteousness ǀ in my ǀ heart:
I have spoken of your faithfulness ǀ and of ǀ your salǀvation.

13 I have not kept back your loving-kindness ǀ and your ǀ truth:
from the ǀ great ǀ congreǀgation.

14 O Lord do not withhold your ǀ mercy ǀ from me:
let your loving-kindness and your ǀ truth ǀ ever · preǀ-serve me.

15 For innumerable troubles have ǀ come upǀon me:
my sins have overtaken me ǀ and I ǀ cannot ǀ see.

16 They are more in number than the ǀ hairs · of my ǀ head:
thereǀfore my ǀ heart ǀ fails me.

17 Be pleased O ǀ Lord · to deǀliver me:
O ǀ Lord make ǀ haste to ǀ help me.

18 Let those who seek my life to ǀ take it · aǀway:
be put to shame and conǀfounded ǀ altoǀgether.

19 Let them be turned back and disgraced who ǀ wish me ǀ evil:
let them be aghast for shame who ǀ say to me · 'Aǀha aǀha!'

20 Let all who seek you be joyful and ǀ glad beǀcause of you:
let those who love your salvation say ǀ always · 'The ǀ Lord is ǀ great.'

21 As for me I am ǀ poor and ǀ needy:
but the ǀ Lord will ǀ care ǀ for me.

†22 You are my helper and ǀ my deǀliverer:
make no long deǀlay O ǀ Lord my ǀ God.

41

1 Blessèd is he that considers the ¦ poor and ¦ helpless:
the Lord will deliver him ¦ in the ¦ day of ¦ trouble.

2 The Lord will guard him and preserve his life
he shall be counted ¦ happy · in the ¦ land:
you will not give him ¦ over · to the ¦ will · of his ¦ enemies.

†3 And if he lies sick on his bed the ¦ Lord · will sus¦tain him:
if illness lays him ¦ low · you will ¦ over¦throw it.

4 I said 'O Lord be ¦ merciful · to¦ward me:
heal me for ¦ I have ¦ sinned a¦gainst you.'

5 My enemies speak evil ¦ of me ¦ saying:
'When will he die and his ¦ name ¦ perish · for ¦ ever?'

6 And if one should come to see me he mouths ¦ empty ¦ words:
while his heart gathers mischief
and ¦ when he · goes ¦ out he ¦ vents it.

7 All those that hate me whisper to¦gether · a¦gainst me:
they de¦vise ¦ plots a¦gainst me.

8 They say 'A deadly ¦ thing has · got ¦ hold of him:
he will not get up a¦gain from ¦ where he ¦ lies.'

9 Even my bosom friend in ¦ whom I ¦ trusted:
who shared my bread has ¦ lifted · his ¦ heel a¦gainst me.

10 But you O Lord be gracious and ¦ raise me ¦ up:
and I will repay them ¦ what they ¦ have de¦served.

11 By this will I ˡ know that · you ˡ favour me:
that my enemy ˡ shall not ˡ triumph ˡ over me.

(†)12 Because of my innocence you ˡ hold me ˡ fast:
you have set me beˡfore your ˡ face for ˡ ever.

(13 Blessèd be the Lord the ˡ God of ˡ Israel:
from everlasting to everlasting * ˡ Amen ˡ A– ˡ men.)

42

1 As a deer longs for the ˡ running ˡ brooks:
so longs my ˡ soul for ˡ you O ˡ God.

2 My soul is thirsty for God * thirsty for the ˡ living ˡ God:
when shall I ˡ come and ˡ see his ˡ face?

3 My tears have been my food ˡ day and ˡ night:
while they ask me all day long ˡ 'Where now ˡ is your ˡ God?'

4 As I pour out my soul by myself I reˡmember ˡ this:
how I went to the house of the Mighty One ˡ‿ into · the ˡ temple · of ˡ God,

†5 To the shouts and ˡ songs of · thanksˡgiving:
a multitude ˡ keeping ˡ high ˡ festival.

6 *Why are you so full of ˡ heaviness · my ˡ soul:*
and ˡ why · so unˡquiet · withˡin me?

7 *O put your ǀ trust in ǀ God:*
for I will praise him yet
who is my de¦liver·er ǀ and my ǀ God.

8 My soul is ǀ heavy · with¦in me:
therefore I will remember you from the land of Jordan
from Mizar a¦mong the ǀ hills of ǀ Hermon.

9 Deep calls to deep in the ǀ roar of · your ǀ waters:
all your waves and ǀ breakers ǀ have gone ǀ over me.

10 Surely the Lord will grant his loving mercy ǀ in the ǀ day-time:
and in the night his song will be with me
a ǀ prayer · to the ǀ God · of my ǀ life.

11 I will say to God my rock 'Why have ǀ you for¦gotten me:
why must I go like a mourner be¦cause the ǀ enemy · op¦presses me?'

†12 Like a sword through my bones my ǀ enemies · have ǀ mocked me:
while they ask me all day long ǀ 'Where now ǀ is your ǀ God?'

13 *Why are you so full of ǀ heaviness · my ǀ soul:*
and ǀ why · so un¦quiet · with¦in me?

14 *O put your ǀ trust in ǀ God:*
for I will praise him yet
who is my de¦liver·er ǀ and my ǀ God.

43

1 Give judgement for me O God
take up my cause against an un|godly | people:
deliver me from de|ceitful · and | wicked | men.

2 For you are God my refuge why have you | turned · me a|way:
why must I go like a mourner‿
be|cause the | enemy · op|presses me?

3 O send out your light and your truth and | let them lead me:
let them guide me to your holy | hill and | to your | dwelling.

4 Then I shall go to the altar of God
to God my joy and | my de|light:
and to the harp I shall sing your | praises · O | God my | God.

5 *Why are you so full of | heaviness · my | soul:*
and | why · so un|quiet · with|in me?

6 *O put your | trust in | God:*
for I will praise him yet
who is my de|liver·er | and my | God.

44

1 We have heard with our ears O God‿
our | fathers · have | told us:
what things you did in their | time · in the | days of |
old;

2 How by your own hand you drove out the nations‿
and | planted · us | in:
how you crushed the peoples
but caused | us to | root and | grow.

3 For it was not by their swords‿
that our fathers took pos|session · of the | land:
nor did their own | arm | get them · the | victory,

4 But your right hand your arm‿
and the | light of · your | countenance:
be|cause · you de|lighted · in | them.

5 You are my | king · and my | God:
who or|dained | victory · for | Jacob.

6 By your power we struck our | ene·mies | through:
in your name we trod down | those that | rose a|gainst
us.

7 For I did not | trust · in my | bow:
nor | could my | sword | save me;

8 But it was you that delivered us | from our | enemies:
and put our | adver·saries | to con|fusion.

†9 In God we made our boast | all the · day | long:
we gave | thanks to · your | name with·out | ceasing.

10 But now you have cast us off and ˈ brought us · to ˈ shame:
you ˈ go not ˈ out · with our ˈ armies.

11 You have caused us to show our ˈ backs · to the ˈ enemy:
so that our foes ˈ plunder ˈ us at ˈ will.

12 You have given us like ˈ sheep · to be ˈ butchered:
you have ˈ scattered us · aˈmong the ˈ nations.

13 You have sold your ˈ people · for ˈ nothing:
and ˈ made a ˈ profit·less ˈ bargain.

14 You have made us a laughing-stock ˈ to our ˈ neighbours:
mocked and held in deˈrision · by ˈ those aˈbout us.

15 You have made us a byword aˈmong the ˈ nations:
so that the peoples ˈ toss their ˈ heads in ˈ scorn.

16 My disgrace is before me ˈ all the ˈ day:
and ˈ shame has ˈ covered · my ˈ face,

17 At the voice of the slanderer ˈ and reˈviler:
at the sight of the ˈ ene·my ˈ and aˈvenger.

18 All this has come upon us though we have ˈ not forˈgotten you:
we have ˈ not beˈtrayed your ˈ covenant.

19 Our hearts have ˈ not turned ˈ back:
nor have our steps ˈ strayed ˈ from your ˈ paths.

20 And yet you have crushed us in the ˈ haunt of ˈ jackals:
and covered us ˈ with the ˈ shadow · of ˈ death.

21 If we had forgotten the ˈ name of · our ˈ God:
or stretched out our hands in ˈ prayer to · some ˈ strange ˈ god,

22 Would not God | search it | out?:
for he knows the very | secrets | of the | heart.

23 But for your sake are we killed | all the · day | long:
we are | counted · as | sheep · for the | slaughter.

24 Rouse yourself O Lord | why · do you | sleep?:
awake do not | cast us | off for | ever.

25 Why do you | hide your | face:
and forget our | misery · and | our af|fliction?

26 Our souls are | bowed · to the | dust:
our | bellies | cleave · to the | ground.

27 Arise O | Lord to | help us:
and redeem us | for your | mercy's | sake.

45

1 My heart is astir with fine phrases
I make my | song · for a | king:
my tongue is the | pen · of a | ready | writer.

2 You are the fairest of the sons of men
grace | flows · from your | lips:
therefore has God | blessed you · for | ever · and | ever.

3 Gird your sword upon your thigh O | mighty | warrior:
in glory and majesty tread | down your | foes and |
triumph!

4 Ride on in the | cause of | truth:
and | for the | sake of | justice.

5 Your right hand shall teach a ˡ terrible · inˡstruction:
peoples shall fall beneath you * your arrows shall be‿
sharp in the ˡ hearts · of the ˡ king's ˡ enemies.

6 Your throne is the throne of God it enˡdures for ˡ
ever:
and the sceptre of your ˡ kingdom · is a ˡ righteous ˡ
sceptre.

7 You have loved righteousness and ˡ hated ˡ evil:
therefore God your God * has anointed you‿
with the oil of ˡ gladness · aˡbove your ˡ fellows.

8 All your garments are fragrant‿
with myrrh ˡ aloes · and ˡ cassia:
music from ivory ˡ pala·ces ˡ makes you ˡ glad.

†9 Kings' daughters are among your ˡ noble ˡ women:
the queen is at your right ˡ hand in ˡ gold of ˡ Ophir.

10 Hear O daughter consider and inˡcline your ˡ ear:
forget your own ˡ people · and your ˡ father's ˡ house.

11 The king deˡsires your ˡ beauty:
he is your lord ˡ therefore · bow ˡ down beˡfore him.

†12 The richest among the people O ˡ daughter · of ˡ Tyre:
shall enˡtreat your ˡ favour · with ˡ gifts.

13 The king's daughter is all ˡ glorious · withˡin:
her clothing is emˡbroidered ˡ cloth of ˡ gold.

14 In robes of many colours she is led to ˡ you O ˡ king:
and after her the ˡ virgins ˡ that are ˡ with her.

†15 They are led with | gladness · and re|joicing:
they enter the | palace | of the | king.

16 In place of your fathers | you shall · have | sons:
and make them princes | over | all the | land.

17 And I will make known your name to every | gener|-ation:
therefore the peoples shall | give you | praise for | ever.

46

1 God is our | refuge · and | strength:
a very | present | help in | trouble.

2 Therefore we will not fear though the | earth be | moved:
and though the mountains are | shaken · in the | midst · of the | sea;

†3 Though the waters | rage and | foam:
and though the mountains quake at the | rising | of the | sea.

4 There is a river whose streams make glad the | city · of | God:
the holy dwelling-place | of the | Most | High.

5 God is in the midst of her
therefore she shall | not be | moved:
God will | help her · and at | break of | day.

6 The nations make uproar and the ˡ kingdoms · are shaken:
but God has lifted his ˡ voice · and the ˡ earth shall tremble.

7 *The Lord of ˡ hosts is ˡ with us:*
the God of ˡ Jacob ˡ is our ˡ stronghold.

8 Come then and see what the ˡ Lord has ˡ done:
what destruction he has ˡ brought upˡon the ˡ earth

9 He makes wars to cease in ˡ all the ˡ world:
he breaks the bow and shatters the spear
and burns the ˡ chari·ots ˡ in the ˡ fire.

10 'Be still and know that ˡ I am ˡ God:
I will be exalted among the nations
I will be exˡalted · upˡon the ˡ earth.'

11 *The Lord of ˡ hosts is ˡ with us:*
the God of ˡ Jacob ˡ is our ˡ stronghold.

47

1 O clap your hands ˡ all you ˡ peoples:
and cry aloud to ˡ God with ˡ shouts of ˡ joy.

2 For the Lord Most High ˡ is to · be ˡ feared:
he is a great ˡ King · over ˡ all the ˡ earth.

3 He cast down ˡ peoples ˡ under us:
and the ˡ nations · beˡneath our ˡ feet.

4 He chose us a land for ˡ our posˡsession:
that was the pride of ˡ Jacob ˡ whom he ˡ loved.

5 God has gone up with the ˡ sound · of reˡjoicing:
and the ˡ Lord · to the ˡ blast · of the ˡ horn.

6 O sing praises sing ˡ praises · to ˡ God:
O sing praises sing ˡ praises ˡ to our ˡ King.

7 For God is the King of ˡ all the ˡ earth:
O ˡ praise him · in a ˡ well-wrought ˡ psalm.

8 God has become the ˡ King · of the ˡ nations:
he has taken his seat upˡon his ˡ holy ˡ throne.

9 The princes of the peoples are ˡ gathered · toˡgether:
with the ˡ people · of the ˡ God of ˡ Abraham.

10 For the mighty ones of the earth‿
are become the ˡ servants · of ˡ God:
and ˡ he is ˡ greatly · exˡalted.

48

1 Great is the Lord and ˡ greatly · to be ˡ praised:
in the ˡ city ˡ of our ˡ God.

2 High and beautiful is his ˡ holy ˡ hill:
it is the ˡ joy of ˡ all the ˡ earth.

†3 On Mount Zion where godhead truly dwells
stands the city of the ˡ Great ˡ King:
God is well known in her palaces ˡ as a ˡ sure deˡfence.

4 For the kings of the ¦ earth as¦sembled:
they gathered to¦gether · and ¦ came ¦ on;

5 They saw they were ¦ struck ¦ dumb:
they were a¦stonished · and ¦ fled in ¦ terror.

6 Trembling took ¦ hold on them · and ¦ anguish:
as on a ¦ woman ¦ in her ¦ travail;

7 Like the breath of the ¦ east ¦ wind:
that ¦ shatters · the ¦ ships of ¦ Tarshish.

8 As we have heard so have we seen‿
in the city of the ¦ Lord of ¦ hosts:
in the city of our God‿
which ¦ God · has es¦tablished · for ¦ ever.

9 We have called to mind your loving-¦kindness · O ¦ God:
in the ¦ midst of ¦ your ¦ temple.

10 As your name is great O God so also ¦ is your ¦ praise:
even to the ¦ ends ¦ of the ¦ earth.

11 Your right hand is full of victory
let Zion's ¦ hill re¦joice:
let the daughters of Judah be ¦ glad‿
be¦cause of · your ¦ judgements.

12 Walk about Zion go round about her‿
and ¦ count · all her ¦ towers:
consider well her ramparts ¦ pass ¦ through her ¦
palaces;

13 That you may tell those who come after that ¦ such is ¦
God:
our God for ever and ever * and ¦ he will ¦ guide us ·
e¦ternally.

49

1 O hear this ¦ all you ¦ peoples:
give ear all you in¦habit·ants ¦ of the ¦ world,

2 All children of men and ¦ sons of ¦ Adam:
both ¦ rich and ¦ poor a¦like.

3 For my mouth shall ¦ speak ¦ wisdom:
and the thoughts of my heart‿
shall be ¦ full of ¦ under¦standing.

4 I will incline my ¦ ear · to a ¦ riddle:
and unfold the mystery to the ¦ sounds ¦ of the ¦ harp.

5 Why should I fear in the ¦ evil ¦ days:
when the wickedness of ¦ my de¦ceivers · sur¦rounds
me,

6 Though they trust to their ¦ great ¦ wealth:
and boast of the a¦bundance ¦ of their ¦ riches?

7 No man may ¦ ransom · his ¦ brother:
or give ¦ God a ¦ price ¦ for him,

8 So that he may ¦ live for ¦ ever:
and ¦ never ¦ see the ¦ grave;

9 For to ransom men's ¦ lives · is so ¦ costly:
that he must a¦bandon ¦ it for ¦ ever.

10 For we see that ¦ wise men ¦ die:
and perish with the foolish and the ignorant ¦
leaving · their ¦ wealth to ¦ others.

†11 The tomb is their home for ever
their dwelling-place throughout ¦ all · gener¦ations:
though they called estates ¦ after · their ¦ own ¦ names.

12 A rich man without ˡ underˡstanding:
is ˡ like the ˡ beasts that ˡ perish.

13 This is the ˡ lot · of the ˡ foolish:
the end of those who are ˡ pleased · with their ˡ own ˡ words.

14 They are driven like sheep into the grave‿
and ˡ death · is their ˡ shepherd:
they slip down ˡ easi·ly ˡ into · the ˡ tomb.

15 Their bright forms shall wear aˡway · in the ˡ grave:
and ˡ lose their ˡ former ˡ glory.

†16 But God will ˡ ransom · my ˡ life:
he will take me ˡ from the ˡ power · of the ˡ grave.

17 Do not fear when a ˡ man grows ˡ rich:
when the ˡ wealth · of his ˡ household · inˡcreases,

18 For he will take nothing aˡway · when he ˡ dies:
nor will his ˡ wealth go ˡ down ˡ after him.

19 Though he counts himself happy ˡ while he ˡ lives:
and praises you ˡ also ˡ when you ˡ prosper,

20 He will go to the company ˡ of his ˡ fathers:
who will ˡ never ˡ see the ˡ light.

†21 A rich man without ˡ underˡstanding:
is ˡ like the ˡ beasts that ˡ perish.

50

1 The Lord our God the | Mighty One · has | spoken:
and summoned the earth
from the rising of the sun to its | setting | in the | west.

2 From Zion | perfect · in | beauty:
God has | shone | out in | glory.

3 Our God is coming he will | not keep | silent:
before him is devouring fire
and | tempest | whirls a|bout him.

4 He calls to the | heavens · a|bove:
and to the earth so | he may | judge his | people.

5 'Gather to | me my | faithful ones:
those who by sacrifice | made a | coven·ant | with me.'

6 The heavens shall pro|claim his | righteousness:
for | God him|self is | judge.

7 'Listen my people and | I will | speak:
O Israel I am God your God and | I will | give my | testimony.

8 'It is not for your sacrifices that | I re|prove you:
for your burnt-|offerings · are | always · be|fore me.

9 'I will take no | bull · from your | farms:
or | he-goat | from your | pens.

10 'For all the beasts of the forest be|long to | me:
and so do the | cattle · up|on the | mountains.

11 'I know all the | birds · of the | air:
and the grasshoppers of the | field are | in my | sight.

12 'If I were hungry I ׀ would not ׀ tell you:
for the whole world is ׀ mine and ׀ all · that is ׀ in it.

13 'Do I eat the ׀ flesh of ׀ bulls:
or ׀ drink the ׀ blood of ׀ goats?

14 'Offer to God a sacrifice of ׀ thanks׀giving:
and pay your ׀ vows · to the ׀ Most ׀ High.

†15 'Call upon me in the ׀ day of ׀ trouble:
I will bring you out and ׀ you shall ׀ glori·fy ׀ me.'

16 But God ׀ says · to the ׀ wicked:
'What have you to do with reciting my laws
or taking my ׀ coven·ant ׀ on your ׀ lips,

17 'Seeing you ׀ loathe ׀ discipline:
and have ׀ tossed my ׀ words be׀hind you?

18 'When you saw a thief you ׀ went a׀long with him:
and you ׀ threw in · your ׀ lot · with ad׀ulterers.

19 'You have loosed your ׀ mouth in ׀ evil:
and your ׀ tongue strings ׀ lies to׀gether.

20 'You sit and speak a׀gainst your ׀ brother:
and slander your ׀ own ׀ mother's ׀ son.

21 'These things you have done and I ׀ held my ׀ tongue:
and you thought I was just such an׀other ׀ as your׀-
self.

22 'But I ׀ will con׀vict you:
and set before your ׀ eyes what ׀ you have ׀ done.

23 'O consider this you who for׀get ׀ God:
lest I tear you in pieces and ׀ there be ׀ no one · to ׀
save you.

†24 'He honours me who brings sacrifice of ꞁ thanksꞁgiving:
and to him who keeps to my way‿
I will ꞁ show the · salꞁvation · of ꞁ God.'

51

1 Have mercy on me O God in your enꞁduring ꞁ goodness:
according to the fulness of your compassion ꞁ‿
blot out ꞁ my ofꞁfences.

2 Wash me thoroughly ꞁ from my ꞁ wickedness:
and ꞁ cleanse me ꞁ from my ꞁ sin.

3 For I acknowledge ꞁ my reꞁbellion:
and my ꞁ sin is ꞁ ever · beꞁfore me.

4 Against you only have I sinned
and done what is evil ꞁ in your ꞁ eyes:
so you will be just in your sentence
and ꞁ blameless ꞁ in your ꞁ judging.

5 Surely in wickedness I was ꞁ brought to ꞁ birth:
and in ꞁ sin my ꞁ mother · conꞁceived me.

6 You that desire truth in the ꞁ inward ꞁ parts:
O teach me wisdom in the secret ꞁ places ꞁ of the ꞁ heart.

7 Purge me with hyssop and I ꞁ shall be ꞁ clean:
wash me and I ꞁ shall be ꞁ whiter · than ꞁ snow.

8 Make me hear of ꞁ joy and ꞁ gladness:
let the bones which ꞁ you have ꞁ broken · reꞁjoice.

9 Hide your ꞁ face · from my ꞁ sins:
and ꞁ blot out ꞁ all · my inꞁiquities.

10 Create in me a clean ˡ heart O ˡ God:
and reˡnew a · right ˡ spirit · withˡin me.

11 Do not cast me ˡ out · from your ˡ presence:
do not take your ˡ holy ˡ spirit ˡ from me.

12 O give me the gladness of your ˡ help aˡgain:
and supˡport me · with a ˡ willing ˡ spirit.

†13 Then will I teach transˡgressors · your ˡ ways:
and sinners shall ˡ turn to ˡ you aˡgain.

14 O Lord God of my salvation deˡliver me · from ˡ bloodshed:
and my ˡ tongue shall ˡ sing of · your ˡ righteousness.

15 O Lord ˡ open · my ˡ lips:
and my ˡ mouth · shall proˡclaim your ˡ praise.

16 You take no pleasure in sacrifice or ˡ I would ˡ give it:
burnt-ˡofferings · you ˡ do not ˡ want.

17 The sacrifice of God is a ˡ broken ˡ spirit:
a broken and contrite heart O God ˡ you will ˡ not deˡspise.

18 In your graciousness do ˡ good to ˡ Zion:
reˡbuild the ˡ walls · of Jeˡrusalem.

19 Then will you delight in right sacrifices
in burnt-offerings ˡ and obˡlations:
then will they offer young ˡ bulls upˡon your ˡ altar.

52

1 Why O man of power do you boast ˡ all the · day ˡ long:
of mischief done to ˡ him · that is ˡ faithful · to ˡ God?

2 You contrive deˡstroying ˡ slanders:
your tongue is like a sharpened ˡ razor ·‿
it ˡ cuts deˡceitfully.

3 You have loved evil ˡ and not ˡ good:
to tell lies ˡ rather · than to ˡ speak the ˡ truth.

4 You love all words that ˡ may do ˡ hurt:
and ˡ every · deˡceit · of the ˡ tongue.

5 But God will deˡstroy you ˡ utterly:
he will snatch you away and pluck you out of your dwelling
he will upˡroot you · from the ˡ land · of the ˡ living.

6 The righteous shall ˡ see it · and ˡ fear:
they shall ˡ laugh you · to ˡ scorn and ˡ say,

†7 'Behold this is the man‿
who did not take ˡ God · for his ˡ strength:
but trusted in the abundance of his riches
and ˡ found his ˡ strength in ˡ slander.'

8 As for me I am like a green olive tree in the ˡ house of ˡ God:
I will trust in the goodness of ˡ God for ˡ ever · and ˡ ever.

9 I will always give you thanks * for this was ˡ your ˡ doing:
I will glorify your name before the faithful
for ˡ it is ˡ good to ˡ praise you.

53

1 The fool has said in his heart 'There | is no | God':
they have all become vile and abominable in their wickedness
there | is not | one that · does | good.

2 God looked down from heaven upon the | children · of | men:
to see if there were any who would act | wisely ·‿
and | seek · after | God.

3 But they have all turned aside
they have all alike be|come cor|rupt:
there is none that does | good | no not | one.

4 Are all the evildoers devoid of | under|standing:
who eat up my people as men eat bread
and | do not | pray to | God?

5 They shall be | struck with | terror:
for God will scatter the | bones | of the · un|godly.

6 They shall be | put to · con|fusion:
because | God | has re|jected them.

†7 O that deliverance for Israel might come | forth from | Zion:
when the Lord turns again the fortunes of his people
then shall Jacob re|joice and | Israel · be | glad.

54

1 Save me O God by the | power of · your | name:
and | vindicate · me | by your | might.

2 Hear my | prayer O | God:
and | listen · to the | words of · my | mouth.

3 For the insolent have | risen · a|gainst me:
ruthless men who have not set God be|fore them |‿
seek my | life.

4 But surely | God is · my | helper:
the Lord is the up|holder | of my | life.

[5 Let evil recoil on those that | would way|lay me:
O de|stroy them | in your | faithfulness!]

6 Then will I offer you sacrifice with a | willing | heart:
I will praise your name O | Lord for | it is | good.

†]7 For you will deliver me from | every | trouble:
my eyes shall see the | downfall | of my | enemies.

55

1 Hear my | prayer O | God:
and do not hide your|self from | my pe|tition.

2 Give heed to | me and | answer me:
I am | restless · in | my com|plaining.

3 I am in turmoil at the | voice · of the | enemy:
at the | onslaught | of the | wicked.

4 For they bring down dis|aster · up|on me:
they persecute | me with | bitter | fury.

5 My heart | writhes with|in me:
and the terrors of | death have | fallen · up|on me.

6 Fear and trembling | come up|on me:
and | horror | over|whelms me.

7 And I said 'O for the | wings · of a | dove:
that I might fly a|way and | find | rest.

8 'Then I would | flee far | off:
and make my | lodging | in the | wilderness.

9 'I would hasten to | find me · a | refuge:
out | of the | blast of | slander,

10 'Out of the tempest of their | calumny · O | Lord:
and | far · from their | double | tongues.'

11 For I have seen violence and | strife · in the | city:
day and night they go | round it · up|on its | walls.

12 Evil and wickedness | are with|in it:
iniquity is within it
oppression and fraud do | not de|part · from its streets.

13 It was not an enemy that reviled me
or I | might have | borne it:
it was not my foe that dealt so insolently with me
or I might have | hidden · my|self | from him;

14 But it was you a | man · like my|self:
my companion | and · my fam|iliar | friend.

†15 Together we en|joyed sweet | fellowship:
in the | house | of our | God.

[16 Let them pass a|way · in con|fusion:
let death | carry · them | to des|truction;

17 Let them go down a|live to | Sheol:
for evil is a|mong them | in their | dwellings.]

18 But I will | call to | God:
and the | Lord my | God will | save me.

19 At evening at morning | and at | noon-day:
I com|plain and | groan a|loud.

20 And he will | hear my | voice:
and | ransom · my | soul in | peace,

21 From those that bear | down up|on me:
for | there are | many · a|gainst me.

22 God will hear and | bring them | low:
he that | is en|throned for | ever.

23 For they do not | keep their | word:
and they | have no | fear of | God.

24 They lay violent hands‿
on those that | are at | peace with them:
they | break | solemn | covenants.

25 Their mouths are smooth as butter
but war is | in their | hearts:
their words are softer than oil
yet | they are | drawn | swords.

26 Cast your burden on the Lord and | he · will sus|tain
you:
he will never suffer the | righteous | man to | stumble.

27 But as for them you will bring them | down O | God:
even | to the | depths · of the | Pit.

†28 Bloodthirsty and deceitful men‿
shall not live out ¦ half their ¦ days:
but ¦ I will ¦ trust in ¦ you.

56

1 Be merciful to me O God for men are ¦ treading · me ¦ down:
all day long my ¦ adver·sary ¦ presses · up¦on me.

2 My enemies tread me down ¦ all the ¦ day:
for there are many that ¦ arrogant·ly ¦ fight a¦gainst me.

3 In the ¦ hour of ¦ fear:
I will ¦ put my ¦ trust in ¦ you.

4 In God whose word I praise * in God I ¦ trust and ¦ fear not:
what can ¦ flesh ¦ do to ¦ me?

5 All day long they afflict me ¦ with their ¦ words:
and every thought is ¦ how to ¦ do me ¦ evil.

6 They stir up hatred ¦ and con¦ceal themselves:
they watch my steps while they ¦ lie in ¦ wait for · my ¦ life.

7 Let there be ¦ no es¦cape for them:
bring down the ¦ peoples · in your ¦ wrath O ¦ God.

8 You have counted my anxious tossings
put my | tears · in your | bottle:
are not these things | noted | in your | book?

9 In the day that I call to you my enemies shall | turn | back:
this I | know for | God is | with me.

10 In God whose word I praise * in God I | trust and | fear not:
what can | man | do to | me?

11 To you O God must I per|form my | vows:
I will pay the thank-|offer·ing | that is | due.

12 For you will deliver my soul from death‿
and my | feet from | falling:
that I may walk before | God · in the | light · of the | living.

57

1 Be merciful to me O | God be | merciful:
for I | come to | you for | shelter;

2 And in the shadow of your wings will | I take | refuge:
until these | troubles · are | over-|past.

3 I will call to | God Most | High:
to the God who will ful|fil his | purpose | for me.

4 He will send from | heaven · and | save me:
he will send forth his faithfulness and his loving-kindness
and rebuke | those · that would | trample · me | down.

5 For I lie amidst ˈ raven·ing ˈ lions:
men whose teeth are spears and arrows
and their ˈ tongue a ˈ sharpened ˈ sword.

6 *Be exalted O God aˈbove the ˈ heavens:*
and let your glory be ˈ over ˈ all the ˈ earth.

7 They have set a net for my feet and I am ˈ brought low:
they have dug a pit before me
but shall ˈ fall · into ˈ it themˈselves.

8 My heart is fixed O God my ˈ heart is ˈ fixed:
I will ˈ sing and ˈ make ˈ melody.

9 Awake my soul awake ˈ lute and ˈ harp:
for ˈ I · will aˈwaken · the ˈ morning.

10 I will give you thanks O Lord aˈmong the ˈ peoples:
I will sing your ˈ praise aˈmong the ˈ nations.

11 For the greatness of your mercy ˈ reaches · to the heavens:
and your ˈ faithful·ness ˈ to the ˈ clouds.

12 *Be exalted O God aˈbove the ˈ heavens:*
and let your glory be ˈ over ˈ all the ˈ earth.

58

[1 Do you indeed decree what is ˈ just O ˈ rulers:
do you with uprightness ˈ judge the ˈ children · of men?

2 No you work in the land with ¦ evil ¦ heart:
you look on the violence ¦ that your ¦ hands have ¦ wrought.

3 The wicked are estranged ¦ even · from the ¦ womb:
they are liars that go a¦stray ¦ from their ¦ birth.

4 They are venomous with the ¦ venom · of ¦ serpents:
like the deaf ¦ asp that ¦ stops its ¦ ears,

†5 And will not heed the ¦ voice · of the ¦ charmers:
though the ¦ binder · of ¦ spells be ¦ skilful.

6 Break their teeth O ¦ God · in their ¦ mouths:
shatter the jaws of the ¦ young ¦ lions · O ¦ Lord.

7 Let them dissolve and drain a¦way like ¦ water:
let them be trodden down ¦ let them ¦ wither · like ¦ grass,

8 Like a woman's miscarriage that melts and ¦ passes · a¦way:
like an abortive birth that ¦ has not ¦ seen the ¦ sun.

9 Before they know it let them be cut ¦ down like ¦ thorns:
like brambles which a ¦ man sweeps ¦ angrily · a¦side.

10 The righteous shall rejoice when he ¦ sees the ¦ vengeance:
he will wash his feet in the ¦ blood of ¦ the un¦godly.

11 And men will say 'There is re¦ward · for the ¦ righteous:
there is indeed a ¦ God who ¦ judges · on ¦ earth.']

59

1 Deliver me from my ˈ enemies · O ˈ God:
lift me to safety from ˈ those that ˈ rise aˈgainst me;

2 O deliver me from the ˈ evilˈdoers:
and ˈ save me · from ˈ blood·thirsty ˈ men.

3 For they lie in ˈ wait · for my ˈ life:
savage men ˈ stir up ˈ violence · aˈgainst me.

4 Not for my sin or my transgression O Lord
not for any ˈ evil · I have ˈ done:
do they run and take ˈ up poˈsition · aˈgainst me.

(†)5 Arise to ˈ meet me · and ˈ see:
you that are Lord of ˈ hosts and ˈ God of ˈ Israel.

[6 Awake to punish ˈ all the ˈ nations:
have no mercy on those that so ˈ treacherous·ly ˈ do wrong.]

7 They return every evening they ˈ howl like ˈ dogs:
they ˈ prowl aˈround the ˈ city.

8 Look how their ˈ mouths ˈ slaver:
swords strike from their lips
for they ˈ say ˈ 'Who will ˈ hear it?'

9 But you O Lord will ˈ laugh them · to ˈ scorn:
you will deˈride ˈ all the ˈ nations.

10 I will look to ˈ you · O my ˈ strength:
for ˈ God is · my ˈ strong ˈ tower.

11 My God in his steadfastness will ˈ come to ˈ meet me:
God will show me the ˈ downfall ˈ of my ˈ enemies.

12 Slay them not O Lord lest my ǀ people · forǀget:
but make them stagger by your ǀ power and ǀ bring them ǀ down.

13 Give them over to punishment * for the sin of their mouths for the ǀ words of · their ǀ lips:
let them be ǀ taken ǀ in their ǀ pride.

[14 For the curses and lies that they have uttered O consume them ǀ in your ǀ wrath:
consume them ǀ till they ǀ are no ǀ more;]

[†] 15 That men may know that God ǀ rules · over ǀ Jacob:
even to the ǀ ends ǀ of the ǀ earth.

16 They return every evening they ǀ howl like ǀ dogs:
they ǀ prowl aǀround the ǀ city.

17 They roam here and there ǀ looking · for ǀ food:
and ǀ growl · if they ǀ are not ǀ filled.

18 But I will ǀ sing of · your ǀ might:
I will sing aloud each ǀ morning ǀ of your ǀ goodness.

19 For you have been my ǀ strong ǀ tower:
and a sure refuge in the ǀ day of ǀ my disǀtress.

†20 I will sing your praises ǀ O my ǀ strength:
for ǀ God is · my ǀ strong ǀ tower.

60

1 O God you have cast us ˈ off and ˈ broken us:
you were enraged against us ˈ O reˈstore us · aˈgain!

2 You have caused the land to quake you have ˈ rent it ˈ open:
heal the rifts for the ˈ earth ˈ quivers · and ˈ breaks.

3 You have steeped your people in a ˈ bitter ˈ draught:
you have given them a ˈ wine to ˈ make them ˈ stagger.

4 You have caused those that fear you to ˈ take ˈ flight:
so that they ˈ run ˈ from the ˈ bow.

†5 O save us by your right ˈ hand and ˈ answer us:
that those whom you ˈ love may ˈ be deˈlivered.

6 God has said in his ˈ holy ˈ place:
'I will exult and divide Shechem
I will parcel ˈ out the ˈ valley · of ˈ Succoth.

7 'Gilead is mine and Maˈnasseh · is ˈ mine:
Ephraim is my helmet and ˈ Judah · my ˈ rod · of comˈmand.

†8 'Moab is my wash-bowl over Edom will I ˈ cast my ˈ shoe:
against Philistia ˈ will I ˈ shout in ˈ triumph.'

9 Who will lead me into the ˈ forti·fied ˈ city:
who will ˈ bring me ˈ into ˈ Edom?

10 Have you not cast us ˈ off O ˈ God?:
you ˈ go not ˈ out · with our ˈ armies.

11 Give us your help a|gainst the | enemy:
for | vain · is the | help of | man.

12 By the power of our God we | shall do | valiantly:
for it is he that will | tread | down our | enemies.

61

1 Hear my loud | crying · O | God:
and give | heed | to my | prayer.

2 From the ends of the earth I call to you‿
when my | heart | faints:
O set me on the | rock · that is | higher · than | I.

3 For you have | been my | refuge:
and my strong | tower a|gainst the | enemy.

4 I will dwell in your | tent for | ever:
and find shelter in the | cover·ing | of your | wings.

5 For you have heard my | vows O | God:
you have granted the desire of | those that | fear your | name.

6 You will give the | king long | life:
and his years shall endure through | many | gener|a-tions.

7 He shall dwell before | God for | ever:
loving-kindness and | truth shall | be his | guard.

8 So will I ever sing praises | to your | name:
while I | daily · per|form my | vows.

62

1 My soul waits in ǀ silence · for ǀ God:
for from ǀ him comes ǀ my salǀvation.

2 He only is my rock and ǀ my salǀvation:
my strong tower so that ǀ I shall ǀ never · be ǀ moved.

3 How long will you all plot against a ǀ man · to deǀstroy him:
as though he were a leaning ǀ fence · or a ǀ buckling ǀ wall?

4 Their design is to thrust him from his height
and their deǀlight · is in ǀ lies:
they bless with their ǀ lips but ǀ inwardly · they ǀ curse.

5 Nevertheless my soul wait in ǀ silence · for ǀ God:
for from ǀ him ǀ comes my ǀ hope.

6 He only is my rock and ǀ my salǀvation:
my strong tower so that ǀ I shall ǀ not be ǀ moved.

7 In God is my deliverance ǀ and my ǀ glory:
God is my strong ǀ rock ǀ and my ǀ shelter.

8 Trust in him at all times ǀ O my ǀ people:
pour out your hearts before him for ǀ God ǀ is our ǀ refuge.

9 The children of men are but breath
the children of ǀ men · are a ǀ lie:
place them in the scales and they fly upward
they ǀ are as ǀ light as ǀ air.

10 Put no trust in extortion
do not grow | worthless · by | robbery:
if riches increase | set not · your | heart up|on them.

11 God has spoken once twice have I | heard him | say:
that | power be|longs to | God,

12 That to the Lord belongs a | constant | goodness:
for you reward a man ac|cording | to his | works.

63

1 O God | you are · my | God:
eagerly | will I | seek | you.

2 My soul thirsts for you my | flesh | longs for you:
as a dry and thirsty | land · where no | water | is.

3 So it was when I beheld you | in the | sanctuary:
and | saw your | power · and your | glory.

4 For your unchanging goodness is | better · than | life:
there|fore my | lips shall | praise you.

5 And so I will bless you as | long as · I | live:
and in your name will I | lift my | hands on | high.

6 My longing shall be satisfied‿
as with | marrow · and | fatness:
my mouth shall | praise you · with ex|ultant | lips.

7 When I remember you up|on my | bed:
when I meditate up|on you · in the | night | watches,

8 How you have | been my | helper:
then I sing for joy in the | shadow | of your | wings,

†9 Then my ˡ soul ˡ clings to you:
and ˡ your right ˡ hand upˡholds me.

10 Those that seek my life are ˡ marked · for deˡstruction:
they shall go down to the deep ˡ places ˡ of the ˡ earth.

11 They shall be deˡlivered · to the ˡ sword:
they shall ˡ be a ˡ portion · for ˡ jackals.

†12 The king will rejoice in God
and all who take oaths on his ˡ name shall ˡ glory:
but the mouths of ˡ liars ˡ shall be ˡ stopped.

64

1 Hear my voice O God in ˡ my comˡplaining:
preserve my ˡ life from ˡ fear · of the ˡ enemy.

2 Hide me from the conspiracy ˡ of the ˡ wicked:
from the ˡ throng of ˡ evilˡdoers,

3 Who sharpen their ˡ tongues like ˡ swords:
who string the bow who take ˡ arrows · of ˡ bitter ˡ
words,

4 To shoot from hiding at the ˡ blameless ˡ man:
to strike at him ˡ sudden·ly ˡ and unˡseen.

5 They are confirmed in an ˡ evil ˡ purpose:
they confide it to one another while they lay the‿
snares ˡ saying ˡ 'Who will ˡ see them?'

6 They hatch mischief they hide a well-conˡsidered ˡ
plan:
for the mind and heart of ˡ man is ˡ very ˡ deep.

7 But God will shoot at them with his ˡ swift ˡ arrows:
they shall be ˡ sudden·ly ˡ struck ˡ through.

8 The Lord will bring them down‿
for what their ˡ tongues have ˡ spoken:
and all that see it shall ˡ toss their ˡ heads in ˡ scorn.

9 Then ˡ all men · shall ˡ fear:
and tell what the Lord has ˡ done and ˡ ponder · his ˡ works.

10 The righteous man shall rejoice in the Lord
and find in ˡ him his ˡ refuge:
and all the ˡ upright · in ˡ heart · shall exˡult.

65

1 You are to be praised O ˡ God in ˡ Zion:
to you shall vows be paid ˡ you that ˡ answer ˡ prayer.

2 To you shall all flesh come to conˡfess their ˡ sins:
when our misdeeds prevail against us ˡ‿
you will ˡ purge · them aˡway.

†3 Blessèd is the man whom you choose
and take to yourself to dwell withˡin your ˡ courts:
we shall be filled with the good things‿
of your house ˡ of your ˡ holy ˡ temple.

4 You will answer us in your righteousness‿
with terrible deeds O ˡ God our ˡ saviour:
you that are the hope of all the ends of the earth‿
and ˡ of the ˡ distant ˡ seas;

5 Who by your strength made ˡ fast the ˡ mountains:
you ˡ that are ˡ girded · with ˡ power;

6 Who stilled the raging of the seas‿
the ˡ roaring · of the ˡ waves:
and the ˡ tumult ˡ of the ˡ peoples.

7 Those who dwell at the ends of the earth‿
are aˡfraid at · your ˡ wonders:
the dawn and the ˡ even·ing ˡ sing your ˡ praises.

8 You tend the ˡ earth and ˡ water it:
you ˡ make it ˡ rich and ˡ fertile.

9 The river of God is ˡ full of ˡ water:
and so providing for the earth‿
you proˡvide ˡ grain for ˡ men.

10 You drench its furrows you level the ˡ ridges · beˡ-
tween:
you soften it with showers and ˡ bless its ˡ early ˡ
growth.

11 You crown the ˡ year · with your ˡ goodness:
and the tracks where you have ˡ passed ˡ drip with ˡ
fatness.

12 The pastures of the ˡ wilderness · run ˡ over:
and the ˡ hills are ˡ girded · with ˡ joy.

13 The meadows are ˡ clothed with ˡ sheep:
and the valleys stand so thick with corn‿
they ˡ shout for ˡ joy and ˡ sing.

66

1 O shout with joy to God | all the | earth:
sing to the honour of his name
and give him | glory | as his | praise.

2 Say to God 'How fearful | are your | works:
because of your great might‿
your | enemies · shall | cower · be|fore you.'

3 All the | earth shall | worship you:
and sing to you and sing | praises | to your | name.

4 Come then and see what | God has | done:
how terrible are his | dealings · with the | children ·
of | men.

5 He turned the sea into dry land
they crossed the | river · on | foot:
then | were we | joyful · be|cause of him.

6 By his power he rules for ever
his eyes keep | watch · on the | nations:
and rebels shall | never | rise a|gainst him.

7 O bless our | God you | peoples:
and cause his | praises | to re|sound,

8 Who has held our | souls in | life:
who has not | suffered · our | feet to | slip.

9 For you have | proved us · O | God:
you have | tried us · as | silver · is | tried.

10 You brought us | into · the | net:
you laid sharp | torment | on our | loins.

†11 You let men ride over our heads
we went through ˡ fire and ˡ water:
but you brought us out ˡ into · a ˡ place of ˡ liberty.

12 I will come into your house with ˡ burnt-ˡofferings:
and ˡ I will ˡ pay you · my ˡ vows,

13 The vows that ˡ opened · my ˡ lips:
that my mouth uttered ˡ when I ˡ was in ˡ trouble.

14 I will offer you burnt-offerings of fattened beasts
with the sweet ˡ smoke of ˡ rams:
I will sacrifice a ˡ bull · and the ˡ flesh of ˡ goats.

15 Come then and hear all ˡ you that · fear ˡ God:
and I will ˡ tell what ˡ he has ˡ done for me.

16 I called to him ˡ with my ˡ mouth:
and his ˡ praise was ˡ on my ˡ tongue.

17 If I had cherished wickedness ˡ in my ˡ heart:
the ˡ Lord would ˡ not have ˡ heard me.

18 But ˡ God has ˡ heard me:
he has ˡ heeded · the ˡ voice of · my ˡ prayer.

19 Praise ˡ be to ˡ God:
who has not turned back my prayer
or his ˡ steadfast ˡ love ˡ from me.

67

1 Let God be gracious to ꞁ us and ꞁ bless us:
and make his ꞁ face ꞁ shine upꞁon us,

2 That your ways may be ꞁ known on ꞁ earth:
your liberating ꞁ power · aꞁmong all ꞁ nations.

3 Let the peoples ꞁ praise you · O ꞁ God:
let ꞁ all the ꞁ peoples ꞁ praise you.

4 Let the nations be ꞁ glad and ꞁ sing:
for you judge the peoples with integrity
and govern the ꞁ nations · upꞁon ꞁ earth.

5 Let the peoples ꞁ praise you · O ꞁ God:
let ꞁ all the ꞁ peoples ꞁ praise you.

6 Then the earth will ꞁ yield its ꞁ fruitfulness:
and ꞁ God our ꞁ God will ꞁ bless us.

†7 God ꞁ shall ꞁ bless us:
and all the ꞁ ends · of the ꞁ earth will ꞁ fear him.

68

1 God shall arise and his enemies ꞁ shall be ꞁ scattered:
those that hate him shall ꞁ flee beꞁfore his ꞁ face.

2 As smoke is dispersed so shall ꞁ they · be disꞁpersed:
as wax melts before a fire
so shall the wicked ꞁ perish · at the ꞁ presence · of ꞁ God.

3 But the righteous shall be glad and ex¦ult be·fore ¦ God:
they ¦ shall re¦joice with ¦ gladness.

4 O sing to God   sing praises ¦ to his ¦ name:
glorify him that rode through the deserts
him whose name is the Lord ¦ and ex¦ult be¦fore him.

5 He is the father of the fatherless
he upholds the ¦ cause · of the ¦ widow:
God ¦ in his ¦ holy ¦ dwelling place.

6 He gives the desolate a home to dwell in
and brings the prisoners out ¦ into · pros¦perity:
but rebels must ¦ dwell · in a ¦ barren ¦ land.

7 O God   when you went out be¦fore your ¦ people:
when you ¦ marched ¦ through the ¦ wilderness,

8 The earth shook   the heavens ¦ poured down ¦ water:
before the God of Sinai   before ¦ God the ¦ God of ¦
Israel.

9 You showered down a generous ¦ rain O ¦ God:
you prepared the land of your pos¦session · when ¦ it
was ¦ weary.

10 And there your ¦ people ¦ settled:
in the place that your goodness O God‿
had made ¦ ready ¦ for the ¦ poor.

11 The Lord spoke the word * and great was the company of those that ¦ carried · the ¦ tidings:
'Kings with their armies are ¦ fleeing · are ¦ fleeing ·
a¦way.

12 'Even the women at home may ¦ share · in the ¦ spoil:
and will you sit ¦ idly · a¦mong the ¦ sheepfolds?

13 'There are images of doves‿
whose wings are ǀ covered · with ǀ silver:
and their ǀ pinions · with ǀ shining ǀ gold.'

14 When the Almighty ǀ scattered ǀ kings:
they were like snow ǀ falling · upǀon Mount ǀ Zalmon.

15 The mountain of Bashan is a ǀ mighty ǀ mountain:
the mountain of Bashan is a ǀ mountain · of ǀ many ǀ peaks.

16 O mountains of many peaks why ǀ look so ǀ enviously:
at the mountain where God is pleased to dwell
where the ǀ Lord · will reǀmain for ǀ ever?

17 The chariots of God are twice ten thousand‿
and ǀ thousands up·on ǀ thousands:
the Lord came from Sinai ǀ into · his ǀ holy ǀ place.

18 When you ascended the heights‿
you led the enemy captive * you received ǀ tribute · from ǀ men:
but rebels shall not ǀ dwell · in the ǀ presence · of ǀ God.

19 Blessèd be the Lord day by day
who bears us ǀ as his ǀ burden:
he is the ǀ God of ǀ our deǀliverance.

20 God is to us a ǀ God who ǀ saves:
by God the Lord do ǀ we esǀcape ǀ death.

[21 But God shall smite the ǀ heads · of his ǀ enemies:
the hairy scalp of ǀ those that ǀ walk · in their ǀ sins.

22 The Lord said 'I will bring them | back from Bashan:
I will bring them a|gain · from the | deep | sea';

[†]23 That you may dip your | feet in | blood:
and the tongues of your | dogs ·
in the | blood of · your | enemies.]

24 Your procession is | seen O | God:
the procession of my | God and | King · in the | sanctuary.

25 The singers go before the mu|sicians · come | after:
and around them the maidens | beating | on the | timbrels.

26 In their choirs they | bless | God:
those that are sprung from the fount of | Israel | ‿ bless the | Lord.

27 There is the little tribe of | Benja·min | leading them:
the throng of the princes of Judah
the princes of | Zebulun · and the | princes · of | Naphtali.

28 Give the command my God * in accordance | with your | power:
that godlike | power where|by you | act for us.

29 Give the command from your temple | at Je|rusalem:
and | kings shall | bring you | tribute.

30 Rebuke the beast of the reeds
the herd of bulls amidst the | brutish | peoples:
tread down those that are greedy for silver
scatter the | peoples · that | relish | war.

31 Let them bring | bronze from | Egypt:
let the hands of the Nubians | carry · it | swiftly · to | God.

32 Sing to God you | kingdoms · of the | earth:
O sing | praises | to the | Lord,

33 To him that rides upon the highest heavens that were | from · the be|ginning:
who utters his voice which | is a | mighty | voice.

34 Ascribe power to God whose majesty is | over | Israel:
and his | might is | in the | clouds.

35 Terrible is God who comes from his | holy | place:
the God of Israel who gives‿
power and strength to his people |
Blessèd | be | God.

69

1 Save | me O | God:
for the waters have come up | even | to my | throat.

2 I sink in the deep mire | where no | footing is:
I have come into deep waters | and the | flood sweeps | over me.

3 I am weary with crying out my | throat is | parched:
my eyes fail with | watching · so | long · for my | God.

4 Those that hate me without cause
are more in number than the ǀ hairs · of my ǀ head
those that would destroy me are many
they oppose me wrongfully
for I must restore ǀ things · that I ǀ never ǀ took

5 O God you ǀ know my ǀ foolishness:
and my ǀ sins · are not ǀ hidden ǀ from you.

6 Let not those who wait for you‿
be shamed because of me
O Lord ǀ God of ǀ hosts:
let not those who seek you‿
be disgraced on ǀ my account ·‿
O ǀ God of ǀ Israel.

7 For your sake have I ǀ suffered · re'proach:
and ǀ shame has ǀ covered · my ǀ face.

8 I have become a stranger ǀ to my ǀ brothers:
an alien ǀ to my · own ǀ mother's ǀ sons.

9 Zeal for your house has ǀ eaten · me ǀ up:
and the taunts of those who taunt ǀ you have
fallen · on ǀ me.

10 I afflicted my'self with ǀ fasting:
and that was ǀ turned to ǀ my re'proach.

11 I made ǀ sackcloth · my ǀ clothing:
and I be'came a ǀ byword ǀ to them.

12 Those who sit in the gate ǀ talk of ǀ me:
and the ǀ drunkards · make ǀ songs a'bout me.

13 But to you Lord I ǀ make my ǀ prayer:
at ǀ an ac'cepta·ble ǀ time.

14 Answer me O God in your a|bundant | goodness:
and | with your | sure de|liverance.

15 Bring me out of the mire so that I | may not | sink:
let me be delivered from my enemies‿
and | from the | deep | waters.

16 Let not the flood overwhelm me
or the depths | swallow · me | up:
let not the | Pit · shut its | mouth up|on me.

17 Hear me O Lord as your loving-|kindness · is | good:
turn to me as | your com|passion · is | great.

18 Do not hide your | face · from your | servant:
for I am in trouble | O be | swift to | answer me!

19 Draw near to me | and re|deem me:
O | ransom me · be|cause of · my | enemies!

20 You know | all their | taunts:
my adversaries are | all | in your | sight.

21 Insults have | broken · my | heart:
my shame and dis|grace are | past | healing.

22 I looked for someone to have pity on me
but | there was | no man:
for some to | comfort me · but | found | none.

†23 They gave me | poison · for | food:
and when I was thirsty they | gave me | vinegar · to | drink.

[24 Let their table be|come a | snare:
and their sacri|fici·al | feasts a | trap.

25 Let their eyes be darkened so that they | cannot | see:
and make their | loins | shake con|tinually.

26 Pour out your ¦ wrath up¦on them:
and let your fierce ¦ anger ¦ over¦take them.

27 Let their ¦ camp be ¦ desolate:
and let ¦ no man ¦ dwell · in their ¦ tents.

28 For they persecute him whom ¦ you have ¦ stricken:
and multiply the pain of ¦ him whom ¦ you have wounded.

29 Let them have punishment up¦on ¦ punishment:
let them ¦ not re¦ceive · your for¦giveness.

†30 Let them be blotted out of the ¦ book · of the ¦ living
let them not be written ¦ down a¦mong the righteous.]

31 As for me I am ¦ poor · and in ¦ misery:
O God let your de¦liver·ance ¦ lift me ¦ up.

32 And I will praise the name of ¦ God · in a ¦ song:
and ¦ glori·fy ¦ him with ¦ thanksgiving.

33 And that will please the Lord ¦ more · than an ¦ ox:
more than a bull with ¦ horns and ¦ cloven ¦ hoof.

34 Consider this you that are ¦ meek · and re¦joice:
seek God and ¦ let your ¦ heart be ¦ glad.

35 For the Lord ¦ listens · to the ¦ poor:
he does not despise his ¦ servants ¦ in cap¦tivity.

36 Let the heavens and the ¦ earth ¦ praise him:
the ¦ seas and ¦ all that ¦ moves in them.

37 For God will ¦ save ¦ Zion:
he will re¦build the ¦ cities · of ¦ Judah.

38 His people shall live there and possess it
the seed of his servants ǀ shall inǀherit it:
and those who ǀ love his ǀ name shall ǀ dwell in it.

70

1 O God be ǀ pleased · to deǀliver me:
O ǀ Lord make ǀ haste to ǀ help me.

2 Let them be put to shame and confounded who ǀ seek my ǀ life:
let them be turned back and disǀgraced who ǀ wish me ǀ evil.

3 Let them turn aǀway for ǀ shame:
who ǀ say to me · 'Aǀha aǀha!'

4 Let all who seek you be joyful and ǀ glad beǀcause of you:
let those who love your salvation say ǀ always ǀ 'God is ǀ great.'

5 As for me I am ǀ poor and ǀ needy:
O ǀ God be ǀ swift to ǀ save me.

6 You are my helper and ǀ my deǀliverer:
O ǀ Lord make ǀ no deǀlay.

71

1 To you Lord have I ǀ come for ǀ shelter:
let me ǀ never · be ǀ put to ǀ shame.

2 In your righteousness rescue ǀ and deǀliver me:
incline your ǀ ear to ǀ me and ǀ save me.

3 Be for me a rock of refuge * a fortress | to de|fend me:
for you are my high | rock | and my | stronghold.

4 Rescue me O my God from the | hand · of the | wicked:
from the grasp of the | piti·less | and un|just.

5 For you Lord | are my | hope:
you are my confidence O | God · from my | youth |
upward.

6 On you have I | leaned · since my | birth:
you are he that brought me out of my mother's womb
and my | praise · is of | you con|tinually.

7 I have become as a fearful | warning · to | many:
but | you are · my | strength · and my | refuge.

8 My mouth shall be | filled · with your | praises:
I shall sing of your | glory | all the · day | long.

9 Cast me not away in the | time of · old | age:
nor forsake me | when my | strength | fails.

10 For my enemies | speak a|gainst me:
and those that watch for my life‿
con|spire to|gether | saying,

†11 'God | has for|saken him:
pursue him take him for | there is | none to | save
him.'

12 Be not far | from me · O | God:
my | God make | haste to | help me.

13 Let my adversaries be confounded and | put to | shame:
let those who seek my hurt‿
be | covered · with | scorn · and dis|grace.

14 As for me I will wait in ˈ hope conˈtinually:
and I will ˈ praise you ˈ more and ˈ more.

15 My mouth shall speak of your righteousness ˈ all the ˈ day:
and tell of your salvation ˈ though it · exˈceeds my ˈ telling.

16 I will begin with the mighty acts of the ˈ Lord my ˈ God:
and declare your righteous ˈ dealing ˈ yours aˈlone.

17 O God you have taught me from my ˈ youth ˈ upward:
and to this day I proˈclaim your ˈ marvel·lous ˈ works.

18 Forsake me not O God in my old age when I am ˈ grey-ˈheaded:
till I have shown the strength of your arm‿
to future generations * and your ˈ might to ˈ those‿ that · come ˈ after.

19 Your righteousness O God ˈ reaches · to the ˈ heavens:
great are the things that you have done
O ˈ God ˈ who is ˈ like you?

20 You have burdened me with many and bitter troubles
O ˈ turn · and reˈnew me:
and raise me up aˈgain · from the ˈ depths · of the ˈ earth.

21 Bless me beyond my ˈ former ˈ greatness:
O ˈ turn to me · aˈgain and ˈ comfort me.

22 Then will I praise you upon the lute‿
for your faithfulness ˈ O my ˈ God:
and sing your praises to the harp O ˈ Holy ˈ One of ˈ Israel.

23 My lips shall re|joice in · my | singing:
and my soul | also · for | you have | ransomed me.

†24 My tongue shall speak of your righteous dealing |
all the · day | long:
for they shall be put to shame and disgraced‿
that | seek to | do me | evil.

72

1 Give the king your | judgement · O | God:
and your righteousness to the | son | of a | king,

2 That he may judge your | people | rightly:
and the | poor · of the | land with | equity.

3 Let the mountains be laden with peace‿
be|cause of · his | righteousness:
and the hills also with pros|peri·ty | for his | people.

4 May he give justice to the poor a|mong the | people:
and rescue the children of the | needy ·
and | crush · the op|pressor.

5 May he live while the | sun en|dures:
and while the moon gives light through|out all |
gener|ations.

6 May he come down like rain upon the | new-mown |
fields:
and as | showers · that | water · the | earth.

7 In his time shall | righteous·ness | flourish:
and abundance of peace till the | moon shall | be no |
more.

8 His dominion shall stretch from | sea to | sea:
from the Great | River · to the | ends · of the | earth.

9 His adversaries shall bow | down be|fore him:
and his | enemies · shall | lick the | dust.

10 The kings of Tarshish and of the isles‿
shall | bring | tribute:
the kings of Sheba and | Seba · shall | offer | gifts.

†11 All kings shall fall | down be|fore him:
and all | nations | do him | service.

12 He will deliver the needy | when they | cry:
and the | poor man · that | has no | helper.

13 He will pity the helpless | and the | needy:
and | save the | lives · of the | poor.

†14 He will redeem them from op|pression · and |
violence:
and their blood shall be | precious | in his | sight.

15 Long may he live and be given of the | gold of | Sheba:
may prayer be made for him continually
and men | bless him | every | day.

16 Let there be abundance of | wheat · in the | land:
let it | flourish · on the | tops · of the | mountains;

†17 Let its ears grow fat like the | grain of | Lebanon:
and its sheaves | thicken · like the | grass · of the |
field.

18 Let his name | live for | ever:
and en|dure as | long · as the | sun.

19 Let all peoples use his ' name in ' blessing:
and all ' nations ' call him ' blessèd.

(20 Blessèd be the Lord God the ' God of ' Israel:
who a'lone does ' great ' wonders.

21 Blessèd be his glorious ' name for ' ever:
and let the whole earth be filled with his glory '
Amen'A–'men.)

73

1 God is indeed ' good to ' Israel:
to ' those whose ' hearts are ' pure.

2 Nevertheless my feet were ' almost ' gone:
my ' steps had ' well-nigh ' slipped.

3 For I was filled with envy ' at the ' boastful:
when I saw the un'godly · had ' such tran'quillity.

4 For they ' suffer · no ' pain:
and their ' bodies · are ' hale and ' fat.

5 They come to no mis'fortune · like ' other folk:
nor ' are they ' plagued like ' other men.

6 Therefore they put on ' pride · as a ' necklace:
and clothe themselves in ' vio·lence ' as · in a ' garment.

7 Their eyes shine from ' folds of ' fatness:
and they have ' all that ' heart could ' wish.

8 Their talk is ' malice · and ' mockery:
and they hand down ' slanders ' from on ' high.

9 Their mouths blas¦pheme a·gainst ¦ heaven:
and their tongues go ¦ to and ¦ fro on ¦ earth.

10 Therefore my ¦ people ¦ turn to them:
and ¦ find in ¦ them no ¦ fault.

11 They say ¦ 'How can · God ¦ know:
is there under¦standing · in the ¦ Most ¦ High?'

12 Behold ¦ these are · the un¦godly:
yet they ¦ prosper · and in¦crease in ¦ riches.

13 Was it for nothing then that I ¦ cleansed my ¦ heart:
and ¦ washed my ¦ hands in ¦ innocence?

14 Have I been stricken all day ¦ long in ¦ vain:
and re¦buked ¦ every ¦ morning?

†15 If I had said ¦ 'I will · speak ¦ thus':
I should have betrayed the ¦ fami·ly ¦ of your ¦ children.

16 Then I thought to under¦stand ¦ this:
but it ¦ was too ¦ hard ¦ for me,

17 Till I went into the ¦ sanctuary · of ¦ God:
and then I under¦stood · what their ¦ end will ¦ be.

18 For you set them in ¦ slipper·y ¦ places:
and cause them to ¦ fall · from their ¦ treacher·ous ¦ footholds.

19 How suddenly they are ¦ laid ¦ waste:
they come to an ¦ end they ¦ perish · in ¦ terror.

†20 As with a dream when ¦ one a¦wakes:
so when you rouse yourself O Lord ¦ ‿
you will · de¦spise their ¦ image.

21 When my ¦ heart was ¦ soured:
and I was ¦ wounded ¦ to the ¦ core,

22 I was but ꞁ brutish · and ꞁ ignorant:
no ꞁ better · than a ꞁ beast beꞁfore you.

23 Nevertheless I am ꞁ always ꞁ with you:
for you hold me ꞁ by my ꞁ right ꞁ hand.

24 You will guide me ꞁ with your ꞁ counsel:
and afterwards ꞁ you will ꞁ lead me · to ꞁ glory.

25 Whom have I in ꞁ heaven · but ꞁ you?:
and there is no one upon earth‿
that I deꞁsire · in comꞁparison · with ꞁ you.

26 Though my flesh and my ꞁ heart ꞁ fail me:
you O ꞁ God · are my ꞁ portion · for ꞁ ever.

27 Behold those who forꞁsake you · shall ꞁ perish:
and all who whore after other ꞁ gods you ꞁ will deꞁstroy.

28 But it is good for me to draw ꞁ near to ꞁ God:
I have made the Lord God my refuge
and I will tell of ꞁ all that ꞁ you have ꞁ done.

74

1 O Lord our God why cast us ꞁ off so ꞁ utterly:
why does your anger burn aꞁgainst the ꞁ sheep of ·
your ꞁ pasture?

2 Remember your congregation * whom you took‿
to yourꞁself of ꞁ old:
the people that you redeemed to be‿
your own possession
and Mount ꞁ Zion · where ꞁ you have ꞁ dwelt.

3 Rouse yourself and go to the ǀ utter ǀ ruins:
to all the harm that the ǀ enemy · has ǀ done · in the ǀ sanctuary.

4 Your adversaries have made uproar
in the place appointed ǀ for your ǀ praise:
they have set ǀ up their ǀ standards · in ǀ triumph.

5 They have destroyed on ǀ every ǀ side:
like those who take axes ǀ up · to a ǀ thicket · of ǀ trees.

6 All the carved woodwork they have ǀ broken ǀ down:
and ǀ smashed it · with ǀ hammers · and ǀ hatchets.

7 They have set ǀ fire to · your ǀ sanctuary:
and defiled to the ground the ǀ dwelling- · place ǀ of your ǀ name.

8 They have said in their hearts 'Let us make ǀ havoc ǀ of them':
they have burned down‿
all the holy ǀ places · of ǀ God · in the ǀ land.

9 We see no signs * there is not one ǀ prophet ǀ left:
there is none who knows how ǀ long these ǀ things shall ǀ be.

10 How long shall the adversary ǀ taunt you · O ǀ God:
shall the enemy blas ǀ pheme your ǀ name for ǀ ever?

†11 Why do you hold ǀ back your ǀ hand:
why do you keep your ǀ right hand ǀ in your ǀ bosom?

12 Yet God is my ǀ king · from of ǀ old:
who wrought de ǀ liverance · up ǀ on the ǀ earth.

13 You divided the ꞁ sea · by your ꞁ might:
you shattered the heads of the ꞁ dragons ꞁ in the ꞁ waters.

14 You crushed the ꞁ heads · of Leꞁviathan:
and gave him as food to the ꞁ creatures · of the ꞁ desert ꞁ waste.

15 You cleft open ꞁ spring and ꞁ fountain:
you dried up the ꞁ everꞁflowing ꞁ waters.

16 The day is yours * and so also ꞁ is the ꞁ night:
you have esꞁtablished · the ꞁ moon · and the ꞁ sun.

17 You set all the boundaries ꞁ of the ꞁ earth:
you creꞁated ꞁ winter · and ꞁ summer.

18 Remember O Lord the ꞁ taunts · of the ꞁ enemy:
how a mindless ꞁ people · have blasꞁphemed your ꞁ name.

19 Do not give to the wild beasts the ꞁ soul that ꞁ praises you:
do not forget for ever the ꞁ life of ꞁ your afꞁflicted.

20 Look on all that ꞁ you have ꞁ made:
for it is full of darkness
and ꞁ violence · inꞁhabits · the ꞁ earth.

21 Let not the oppressed and reviled turn aꞁway reꞁjected:
but let the poor and ꞁ needy ꞁ praise your ꞁ name.

22 Arise O God * plead your ꞁ own ꞁ cause:
remember how a mindless people ꞁ taunt you ꞁ all day ꞁ long.

23 Do not forget the ꞁ clamour · of your ꞁ adversaries:
or how the shouting of your ꞁ enemies · asꞁcends conꞁtinually.

75

1 We give you thanks O God we ˈ give you ˈ thanks:
we call upon your name
and tell of all the ˈ wonders ˈ you have ˈ done.

2 'I will surely apˈpoint a ˈ time:
when I the ˈ Lord will ˈ judge with ˈ equity.

3 'Though the earth shake and ˈ all who ˈ dwell in it:
it is ˈ I · that have ˈ founded · its ˈ pillars.

4 'I will say to the boasters ˈ "Boast no ˈ more":
and to the wicked ˈ "Do not ˈ flaunt your ˈ horns;

†5 ' "Do not flaunt your ˈ horns so ˈ high:
or speak so ˈ proud and ˈ stiff- ˈnecked." '

6 For there is none from the east or ˈ from the ˈ west:
or from the wilderness ˈ who can ˈ raise ˈ up;

7 But it is God who ˈ is the ˈ judge:
who puts down ˈ one · and exˈalts anˈother.

8 For there is a cup in the ˈ Lord's ˈ hand:
and the wine ˈ foams · and is ˈ richly ˈ mixed;

9 He gives it in turn to each of the ˈ wicked · of the ˈ earth:
they drink it and ˈ drain it ˈ to the ˈ dregs.

10 But I will sing praises to the ˈ God of ˈ Jacob:
I will ˈ glorify · his ˈ name for ˈ ever.

11 All the horns of the ˈ wicked · I will ˈ break:
but the horns of the ˈ righteous · shall be ˈ lifted ˈ
high.

76

1 In Judah | God is | known:
his | name is | great in | Israel.

2 At Salem | is his | tabernacle:
and his | dwelling | is in | Zion.

3 There he broke in pieces the flashing | arrows · of the | bow:
the shield the | sword · and the | weapons · of | battle.

4 Radiant in | light are | you:
greater in majesty | than · the e|ternal | hills.

5 The valiant were dumbfounded they | sleep their | sleep:
and all the men of | war have | lost their | strength.

6 At the blast of your voice O | God of | Jacob:
both horse and | chariot · were | cast a|sleep.

7 Terrible are | you Lord | God:
and who may stand be|fore you · when | you are | angry?

8 You caused your sentence to be | heard from | heaven:
the earth | feared | and was | still,

9 When God a|rose to | judgement:
to | save · all the | meek · of the | earth.

10 For you crushed the | wrath of | man:
you bridled the | remnant | of the | wrathful.

11 O make vows to the Lord your | God and | keep them:
let all around him bring gifts
to him that is | worthy | to be | feared.

12 For he cuts down the | fury · of | princes:
and he is terrible to the | kings | of the | earth.

77

1 I call to my God I cry | out to|ward him:
I call to my God and | surely | he will | answer.

2 In the day of my distress I seek the Lord
I stretch out my hands to | him by | night:
my soul is poured out without ceasing
it re|fuses | all | comfort.

3 I think upon God and | groan a|loud:
I | muse · and my | spirit | faints.

4 You hold my | eyelids | open:
I am so | dazed · that I | cannot | flee.

5 I consider the | times · that are | past:
I remember the | years of | long a|go.

6 At night I am | grieved · to the | heart:
I ponder | and my | spirit · makes | search;

7 'Will the Lord cast us | off for | ever:
will he | show us · his | favour · no | more?

8 'Is his mercy clean | gone for | ever:
and his promise come to an | end for | all · gener|-
ations?

9 'Has God for|gotten · to be | gracious:
has he shut up his | pity | in dis|pleasure?'

10 And I say * 'Has the right hand of the Most High ¦
lost its ¦ strength:
has the ¦ arm · of the ¦ Lord ¦ changed?'

11 I will declare the mighty ¦ acts · of the ¦ Lord:
I will call to ¦ mind your ¦ wonders · of ¦ old.

12 I will think on all that ¦ you have ¦ done:
and ¦ meditate · up¦on your ¦ works.

13 Your way O ¦ God is ¦ holy:
who is so ¦ great a ¦ god as ¦ our God?

14 You are the God that ¦ works ¦ wonders:
you made known your ¦ power a¦mong the ¦ nations;

15 By your mighty arm you re¦deemed your ¦ people:
the ¦ children · of ¦ Jacob · and ¦ Joseph.

16 The waters saw you O God
the waters saw you and ¦ were a¦fraid:
the ¦ depths ¦ also · were ¦ troubled.

17 The clouds poured out water the ¦ heavens ¦ spoke:
and your ¦ arrows ¦ darted ¦ forth.

18 The voice of your thunder was ¦ heard · in the ¦ whirl-
wind:
your lightnings lit the world
the ¦ earth ¦ shuddered · and ¦ quaked.

19 Your way was in the sea * your path in the ¦ great ¦
waters:
and your ¦ footsteps ¦ were not ¦ seen.

20 You led your ¦ people · like ¦ sheep:
by the ¦ hand of ¦ Moses · and ¦ Aaron.

78

1 Give heed to my teaching ˡ O my ˡ people:
incline your ˡ ears · to the ˡ words of · my ˡ mouth;

2 For I will open my ˡ mouth · in a ˡ parable:
and expound the ˡ mysteries · of ˡ former ˡ times.

3 What we have ˡ heard and ˡ known:
what ˡ our foreˡfathers · have ˡ told us,

4 We will not hide from their children
but declare to a generation ˡ yet to ˡ come:
the praiseworthy acts of the Lord
his ˡ mighty · and ˡ wonder·ful ˡ works.

5 He established a law in Jacob
and made a deˡcree in ˡ Israel:
which he commanded our foreˡfathers ·
to ˡ teach their ˡ children,

6 That future generations might know
and the children ˡ yet unˡborn:
that they in turn might ˡ teach it ˡ to their ˡ sons;

7 So that they might put their ˡ confidence · in ˡ God:
and not forget his ˡ works but ˡ keep · his comˡmandments,

8 And not be as their forefathers
a stubborn and reˡbellious · generˡation:
a generation that did not set their heart aright
whose spirit ˡ was not ˡ faithful · to ˡ God.

9 The children of Ephraim ˡ armed · with the ˡ bow:
turned ˡ back · in the ˡ day of ˡ battle.

10 They did not keep God's covenant
they refused to ˈ walk in · his ˈ law:
they forgot what he had done
and the ˈ wonders ˈ he had ˈ shown them.

11 For he did marvellous things‿
in the ˈ sight of · their ˈ fathers:
in the land of Egypt ˈ in the ˈ country · of ˈ Zoan.

12 He divided the sea and ˈ let them · pass ˈ through:
he made the ˈ waters · stand ˈ up · in a ˈ heap.

13 In the daytime he ˈ led them · with a ˈ cloud:
and all night ˈ long · with the ˈ light of ˈ fire.

14 He cleft ˈ rocks · in the ˈ wilderness:
and gave them drink in abundance ˈ‿
as from ˈ springs of ˈ water.

†15 He brought streams ˈ out of · the ˈ rock:
and caused the waters to ˈ flow ˈ down like ˈ rivers.

16 But for all this they sinned yet ˈ more aˈgainst him:
and rebelled against the Most ˈ High ˈ in the ˈ desert.

17 They wilfully put ˈ God · to the ˈ test:
and deˈmanded ˈ food · for their ˈ appetite.

18 They spoke against ˈ God and ˈ said:
'Can God prepare a ˈ table ˈ in the ˈ wilderness?

19 'He indeed struck the rock
so that the waters gushed and the ˈ streams · overˈ-flowed:
but can he also give bread
or provide ˈ meat ˈ for his ˈ people?'

20 When the Lord heard it he was angry
and a fire was kindled a¦gainst ¦ Jacob:
his wrath ¦ blazed a¦gainst ¦ Israel.

21 For they put no ¦ trust in ¦ God:
nor would they be¦lieve his ¦ power to ¦ save.

†22 Then he commanded the ¦ clouds a¦bove:
and ¦ opened · the ¦ doors of ¦ heaven.

23 He rained down manna for ¦ them to ¦ eat:
and ¦ gave them · the ¦ grain of ¦ heaven.

24 So men ate the ¦ bread of ¦ angels:
and he ¦ sent them ¦ food · in a¦bundance.

25 He stirred up the south east ¦ wind · in the ¦ heavens:
and ¦ guided · it ¦ by his ¦ power.

26 He rained down meat upon them ¦ thick as ¦ dust:
and winged ¦ birds · like the ¦ sands · of the ¦ sea.

27 He made them fall into the ¦ midst of · their ¦ camp:
and ¦ all a¦bout their ¦ tents.

28 So they ate and were ¦ well-¦filled:
for he had ¦ given · them ¦ what · they de¦sired.

29 But before they had ¦ satisfied · their ¦ craving:
while the ¦ food was ¦ still in · their ¦ mouths,

30 The anger of God ¦ blazed · up a¦gainst them:
and he slew their strongest men
and laid ¦ low the ¦ youth of ¦ Israel.

31 But for all this they ¦ sinned yet ¦ more:
and ¦ put no ¦ faith · in his ¦ wonders.

32 So he ended their ǀ days · like a ǀ breath:
and their ǀ years with ǀ sudden ǀ terror.

33 When he struck them down ǀ then they ǀ sought him:
they turned and ǀ sought ǀ eagerly · for ǀ God.

34 They remembered that ǀ God · was their ǀ rock:
that God Most ǀ High was ǀ their reǀdeemer.

35 But they lied to him ǀ with their ǀ mouths:
and disǀsembled ǀ with their ǀ tongues;

36 For their hearts were not ǀ fixed upǀon him:
nor ǀ were they ǀ true to · his ǀ covenant.

37 Yet he being merciful
forgave their iniquity and did ǀ not deǀstroy them:
many times he turned his anger aside
and would not ǀ wholly · aǀrouse his ǀ fury.

38 He remembered that they ǀ were but ǀ flesh:
like a wind that passes ǀ and does ǀ not reǀturn.

39 How often they rebelled against him ǀ in the ǀ wilderness:
and ǀ grieved him ǀ in the ǀ desert!

40 Again and again they put ǀ God · to the ǀ test:
and provoked the ǀ Holy ǀ One of ǀ Israel.

41 They did not reǀmember · his ǀ power:
or the day when he reǀdeemed them ǀ from the ǀ enemy;

42 How he wrought his ǀ signs in ǀ Egypt:
his ǀ wonders · in the ǀ country · of ǀ Zoan.

43 For he turned their ǀ rivers · into ǀ blood:
so that they ǀ could not ǀ drink · from the ǀ streams.

44 He sent swarms of | flies · that de|voured them:
and | frogs that | laid them | waste.

45 He gave their | crops · to the | locust:
and the fruits of their | labour | to the | grasshopper.

46 He struck down their | vines with | hailstones:
and their | syco·more | trees with | frost.

47 He gave up their | cattle · to the | hail:
and their | flocks · to the | flash · of the | lightning.

48 He loosed on them the fierceness of his anger
his fury his indignation | and dis|tress:
and these were his | messen·gers | of de|struction.

49 He opened a | path · for his | fury:
he would not spare them from death
but gave | up their | lives · to the | pestilence.

50 He struck down the | firstborn · of | Egypt:
the first-fruits of their manhood | ‿
in the | dwellings · of | Ham.

51 As for his own people he led them | out like | sheep:
and guided them in the | wilder·ness | like a | flock.

52 He led them in safety and they were | not a|fraid:
but the | sea | covered · their | enemies.

53 He brought them to his | holy | land:
to the mountains that his | own right | hand had | won.

54 He drove out the nations before them
and apportioned their lands | as a · pos|session:
and settled the tribes of | Israel | in their | tents.

55 But they rebelled against God Most High‿
and ˡ put him · to the ˡ test:
they would ˡ not oˡbey · his comˡmandments.

56 They turned back and dealt treacherously ˡ‿
like their ˡ fathers:
they turned aside ˡ slack · as an ˡ unstrung ˡ bow.

57 They provoked him to anger with their ˡ heathen ˡ shrines:
and moved him to jealousy ˡ with their ˡ carved ˡ images.

58 God heard and was angry * he utterly reˡjected ˡ Israel:
he forsook the tabernacle at Shiloh
the ˡ tent · where he ˡ dwelt a·mong ˡ men.

59 He gave the ark of his might ˡ into · capˡtivity:
and his glory ˡ into · the ˡ hands · of the ˡ enemy.

60 He delivered his ˡ people · to the ˡ sword:
and was enraged aˡgainst his ˡ own posˡsession.

61 Fire deˡvoured the · young ˡ men:
there was ˡ no one · to beˡwail the ˡ maidens;

62 Their priests ˡ fell · by the ˡ sword:
and there was ˡ none to ˡ mourn · for the ˡ widows.

63 Then the Lord awoke like a ˡ man · out of ˡ sleep:
like a warrior that had been ˡ overˡcome with ˡ wine.

64 He struck the backs of his enemies ˡ as they ˡ fled:
and ˡ put them · to perˡpetu·al ˡ shame.

65 He rejected the ˡ family · of ˡ Joseph:
he reˡfused the ˡ tribe of ˡ Ephraim.

66 But he chose the ǀ tribe of ǀ Judah:
and the hill of ǀ Zion ǀ which he ǀ loved.

67 He built his sanctuary like the ǀ heights of ǀ heaven:
like the earth which ǀ he had ǀ founded · for ǀ ever.

68 He chose ǀ David · his ǀ servant:
and ǀ took him ǀ from the ǀ sheepfolds;

69 He brought him from ǀ following · the ǀ ewes:
to be the shepherd of his people Jacob
and of ǀ Israel · his ǀ own posǀsession.

70 So he tended them with ǀ upright ǀ heart:
and ǀ guided them · with ǀ skilful ǀ hand.

79

1 O God the heathen have ǀ come in·to your ǀ land:
they have defiled your holy temple
they have made Jeǀrusalem · a ǀ heap of ǀ stones.

2 They have given the dead bodies of your servants‿
as food to the ǀ birds · of the ǀ air:
and the flesh of your faithful ones‿
to the wild ǀ beasts ǀ of the ǀ earth.

3 Their blood they have spilt like water‿
on every ǀ side · of Jeǀrusalem:
and ǀ there is ǀ none to ǀ bury them.

4 We have become a mockery ǀ to our ǀ neighbours:
the scorn and ǀ laughing-stock · of ǀ those aǀbout us.

5 How long O Lord shall your anger be ǀ so exǀtreme:
will your jealous ǀ fury ǀ burn like ǀ fire?

6 Pour out your wrath on the nations that | do not | know
you:
on the kingdoms that have not | called up|on your
name.

7 For they have de|voured | Jacob:
and made his | dwelling-place · a | deso|lation.

8 Do not remember against us the sin of | former | times
but let your compassion hasten to meet us
for we are | brought | very | low.

†9 Help us O God our saviour for the | honour · of your
name:
O deliver us and expiate our | sins · for your | name's
sake.

[10 Why should the heathen say | 'Where is · their | God?'
O let vengeance for the blood of your servants‿
that is shed
be shown upon the | nations | in our | sight.]

11 Let the sorrowful sighing of the prisoners | come be|fore
you:
and as your power is great reprieve | those con|-
demned to | die.

[12 For the taunts with which our neighbours‿
have taunted | you O | Lord:
repay them seven times | over | into · their | bosoms.]

13 So we that are your people and the sheep of your pasture
shall give you | thanks for | ever:
we will declare your praise in | every | gener|ation.

80

1 Hear O Shepherd of Israel
you that led ˈ Joseph · like a ˈ flock:
you that are enthroned upon the cherubim ˈ‿
shine ˈ out in ˈ glory;

2 Before Ephraim Benjamin ˈ and Manˈasseh:
stir up your ˈ power and ˈ come to ˈ save us.

†3 *Restore us again O ˈ Lord of ˈ hosts:*
show us the light of your countenance ˈ‿
and we ˈ shall be ˈ saved.

4 O Lord ˈ God of ˈ hosts:
how long will you be ˈ angry · at your ˈ people's ˈ
prayer?

5 You have fed them with the ˈ bread of ˈ tears:
and given them tears to ˈ drink in ˈ good ˈ measure.

6 You have made us the victim ˈ of our ˈ neighbours:
and our ˈ ene·mies ˈ laugh us · to ˈ scorn.

7 *Restore us again O ˈ Lord of ˈ hosts:*
show us the light of your countenance ˈ‿
and we ˈ shall be ˈ saved.

8 You brought a ˈ vine · out of ˈ Egypt;
you drove out the ˈ nations · and ˈ planted · it ˈ in.

9 You cleared the ˈ ground beˈfore it:
and it struck ˈ root and ˈ filled the ˈ land.

10 The hills were ˈ covered · with its ˈ shadow:
and its boughs were like the ˈ boughs · of the ˈ great ˈ
cedars.

11 It stretched out its ˈ branches · to the ˈ sea:
and its tender ˈ shoots · to the ˈ Great ˈ River.

12 Why then have you broken ˈ down its ˈ walls:
so that every passer-ˈby can ˈ pluck its ˈ fruit?

13 The wild boar out of the woods ˈ roots it ˈ up:
and the locusts from the ˈ wild ˈ places · deˈvour it.

14 Turn to us again O ˈ Lord of ˈ hosts:
look ˈ down from ˈ heaven · and ˈ see.

15 Bestow your care upˈon this ˈ vine:
the stock which your ˈ own right ˈ hand has ˈ planted

16 As for those that burn it with fire and ˈ cut it ˈ down:
let them perish‿
at the reˈbuke ˈ of your ˈ countenance.

17 Let your power rest on the man at your ˈ right ˈ hand:
on that son of man whom you ˈ made so ˈ strong ·‿
for yourˈself.

18 And so we shall ˈ not turn ˈ back from you:
give us life and we will ˈ call upˈon your ˈ name.

19 *Restore us again O ˈ Lord of ˈ hosts:*
show us the light of your countenance ˈ‿
and we ˈ shall be ˈ saved.

81

1 O sing joyfully to | God our | strength:
shout in | triumph · to the | God of | Jacob.

2 Make music and | beat up·on the | drum:
sound the | lute and · the mel|odi·ous | harp.

3 Blow the ram's horn at the | new | moon:
and at the full moon | of our | day of | festival.

4 For this was a | statute · for | Israel:
a com|mandment · of the | God of | Jacob,

†5 Which he laid on Joseph as a | solemn | charge:
when he came | out of · the | land of | Egypt.

6 I heard a voice that I had not | known | saying:
'I eased your shoulders of the burden
and your | hands were | freed · from the | load.

7 'You called to me in trouble | and I | rescued you:
I answered you from the secret place of my thunder
I put you to the | test · at the | waters · of | Meribah.

8 'Listen my people and | I · will ad|monish you:
O Israel if | only | you would | hear me.

9 'There shall be no strange | god a|mong you:
nor shall you bow | down · to an | ali·en | god.

†10 'I am the Lord your God
who brought you up from the | land of | Egypt:
open wide your | mouth and | I will | fill it.

11 'But my people would not | listen · to my | voice:
and | Israel | would have | none of me.

12 'So I left them to the stubbornness ˡ of their ˡ hearts:
to walk acˡcording · to their ˡ own deˡsigns.

13 'If only my ˡ people · would ˡ listen:
if Israel ˡ would but ˡ walk in · my ˡ ways,

14 'I would soon put ˡ down their ˡ enemies:
and turn my ˡ hand aˡgainst their ˡ adversaries.

15 'Those that hate the Lord would ˡ cringe beˡfore him:
and their ˡ punishment · would ˡ last for ˡ ever.

16 'But Israel I would feed with the ˡ finest ˡ wheat:
and satisfy you with ˡ honey ˡ from the ˡ rocks.'

82

1 God has stood up in the ˡ council · of ˡ heaven:
in the midst of the ˡ gods ˡ he gives ˡ judgement.

2 'How long will you ˡ judge unˡjustly:
and ˡ favour · the ˡ cause · of the ˡ wicked?

3 'Judge for the ˡ poor and ˡ fatherless:
vindicate the afˡflicted ˡ and opˡpressed.

4 'Rescue the ˡ poor and ˡ needy:
and ˡ save them · from the ˡ hands · of the ˡ wicked.

5 'They do not know they do not understand
they walk aˡbout in ˡ darkness:
all the foundˡations · of the ˡ earth are ˡ shaken.

6 'Therefore I say ˡ "Though · you are ˡ gods:
and all of you ˡ sons · of the ˡ Most ˡ High,

7 ‘ “Nevertheless you shall ǀ die like ǀ man:
and ǀ fall like ǀ one of · the ǀ princes.” ’

8 Arise O God and ǀ judge the ǀ earth:
for you shall take all ǀ nations · as ǀ your posǀsession.

83

1 Hold not your ǀ peace O ǀ God:
O God be not ǀ silent ǀ or unǀmoved.

2 See how your ǀ enemies · make ǀ uproar:
how those that hate you have ǀ lifted ǀ up their ǀ heads.

3 For they lay shrewd plots aǀgainst your ǀ people:
they scheme against ǀ those whom ǀ you have ǀ cherished.

4 ‘Come’ they say ‘let us destroy them
that they may no ǀ longer · be a ǀ nation:
that the very name of Israel may ǀ be reǀmembered · no ǀ more.’

5 With one mind they conǀspire toǀgether:
they ǀ make alǀliance · aǀgainst you,

6 The tribes of Edom ǀ and the ǀ Ishmaelites:
the people of ǀ Moab ǀ and the ǀ Hagarites,

7 Gebal and ǀ Ammon · and ǀ Amalek:
Philistia ǀ and · the inǀhabitants · of ǀ Tyre;

8 Asshur ǀ also · is ǀ joined with them:
and lends a friendly ǀ arm · to the ǀ children · of ǀ Lot.

9 Do to them as you | did to | Midian:
as to Sisera and Jabin | at the | river · of | Kishon

10 Who were de|stroyed at | Endor:
and be|came like | dung · for the | earth.

11 Make their leaders as | Oreb · and | Zeeb:
and all their princes like | Zebah | and Zal|munn

12 Who said 'Let us | take pos|session:
let us | seize the | pastures · of | God.'

13 Make them like | thistledown · my | God:
or like chaff | blown be|fore the | wind.

14 As fire con|suming · a | thicket:
or as flame that | sets the | hillsides · a|blaze,

15 Pursue them | with your | tempest:
and | terrify · them | with your | storm-wind.

16 Cover their faces with | shame O | Lord:
that | they may | seek your | name.

[17 Let them be disgraced and dis|mayed for | ever:
let them | be con|founded · and | perish,]

(†)18 That they may know that you whose | name · is the Lord:
are alone the Most | High · over | all the | earth.

84

1 How lovely | is your | dwelling-place:
O | Lord | God of | hosts!

2 My soul has a desire and longing‿
to enter the | courts · of the | Lord:
my heart and my flesh re|joice · in the | living | God.

3 The sparrow has found her a home
and the swallow a nest where she may | lay her | young:
even your altar O Lord of | hosts my | King ·‿ and my | God.

4 Blessèd are those who | dwell in · your | house:
they will | always · be | praising | you.

5 Blessèd is the man whose | strength · is in | you:
in whose | heart · are the | highways · to | Zion;

6 Who going through the valley of dryness
finds there a spring from | which to | drink:
till the autumn | rain shall | clothe it · with | blessings.

†7 They go from | strength to | strength:
they appear every one of them‿
before the | God of | gods in | Zion.

8 O Lord God of hosts | hear my | prayer:
give | ear O | God of | Jacob.

9 Behold O God | him who · reigns | over us:
and look upon the | face of | your a|nointed.

10 One day in your courts is ˡ better · than a ˡ thousand:
I would rather stand at the threshold of the house‿
of my God
than ˡ dwell · in the ˡ tents of · unˡgodliness.

11 For the Lord God is a rampart and a shield
the Lord gives ˡ favour · and ˡ honour:
and no good thing will he withhold‿
from ˡ those who ˡ walk in ˡ innocence.

†12 O Lord ˡ God of ˡ hosts:
blessèd is the man who ˡ puts his ˡ trust in ˡ you.

85

1 O Lord you were gracious ˡ to your ˡ land:
you reˡstored the ˡ fortunes · of ˡ Jacob.

2 You forgave the iniquity ˡ of your ˡ people:
and ˡ covered ˡ all their ˡ sin.

3 You put aside ˡ all your ˡ wrath:
and turned away from your ˡ fierce ˡ indigˡnation.

4 Return to us again O ˡ God our ˡ saviour:
and ˡ let your ˡ anger ˡ cease from us.

5 Will you be displeased with ˡ us for ˡ ever:
will you stretch out your wrath
from one geneˡration ˡ to anˡother?

6 Will you not give us ˡ life aˡgain:
that your ˡ people ˡ may reˡjoice in you?

†7 Show us your ǀ mercy · O ǀ Lord:
and ǀ grant us ǀ your salǀvation.

8 I will hear what the Lord ǀ God will ǀ speak:
for he will speak peace to his people
to his faithful ones whose ǀ hearts are ǀ turned to ǀ him.

9 Truly his salvation is near to ǀ those that ǀ fear him:
and his ǀ glory · shall ǀ dwell · in our ǀ land.

10 Mercy and truth are ǀ met toǀgether:
righteousness and ǀ peace have ǀ kissed each ǀ other;

11 Truth shall flourish ǀ out of · the ǀ earth:
and righteousness ǀ shall look ǀ down from ǀ heaven.

12 The Lord will also give us ǀ all · that is ǀ good:
and our ǀ land shall ǀ yield its ǀ plenty.

13 For righteousness shall ǀ go beǀfore him:
and tread the ǀ path beǀfore his ǀ feet.

86

1 Incline your ear to me O ǀ God and ǀ answer me:
for ǀ I am ǀ poor · and in ǀ misery.

2 Preserve my life for ǀ I am ǀ faithful:
my God save your servant who ǀ puts his ǀ trust in ǀ you.

3 Be merciful to ǀ me O ǀ Lord:
for I ǀ call to · you ǀ all the · day ǀ long.

4 O make glad the ˡ soul of · your ˡ servant:
for I put my ˡ hope in ˡ you O ˡ Lord.

5 For you Lord are ˡ good · and forˡgiving:
of great and continuing kindness‿
to ˡ all who ˡ call upˡon you.

6 Hear my ˡ prayer O ˡ Lord:
and give heed to the ˡ voice · of my ˡ suppliˡcation

†7 In the day of my trouble I ˡ call upˡon you:
for ˡ you will ˡ surely ˡ answer.

8 Among the gods there is none like ˡ you O ˡ Lord:
nor are there ˡ any ˡ deeds like ˡ yours.

9 All the nations you have made‿
shall come and ˡ worship · beˡfore you:
O Lord they shall ˡ gloriˡfy your ˡ name.

10 For you are great and do ˡ marvel·lous ˡ things:
and ˡ you aˡlone are ˡ God.

11 Show me your way O Lord and I will ˡ walk in · your
truth:
let my heart deˡlight to ˡ fear your ˡ name.

12 I will praise you O Lord my God with ˡ all my ˡ heart
and I will ˡ glorify · your ˡ name for ˡ ever.

13 For great is your abiding ˡ love toˡward me:
and you have delivered my life‿
from the ˡ lowest ˡ depths · of the ˡ grave.

14 Insolent men O God have ˡ risen · aˡgainst me:
a band of ruthless men seek my life
they have not set ˡ God beˡfore their ˡ eyes.

15 But you Lord are a God ˡ gracious · and comˡpassionate:
slow to anger ˡ full of ˡ goodness · and ˡ truth.

16 Turn to me and be merciful
give your ˡ strength · to your ˡ servant:
and ˡ save the ˡ son of · your ˡ handmaid.

17 Show me some token ˡ of your ˡ goodness:
that those who hate me may see it and be ashamed
because you Lord are my ˡ helper ˡ and my ˡ comforter.

87

1 He has founded it upon a ˡ holy ˡ hill:
and the Lord loves the gates of Zion‿
more than ˡ all the ˡ dwellings · of ˡ Jacob.

2 Glorious things shall be ˡ spoken · of ˡ you:
O Zion ˡ city ˡ of our ˡ God.

3 I might speak of my kinsmen in Egypt ˡ or in ˡ Babylon:
in Philistia Tyre or Nubia ˡ where ˡ each was ˡ born.

4 But of Zion it ˡ shall be ˡ said:
many were born in her
he that is Most ˡ High ˡ has esˡtablished her.

5 When the Lord draws up the record ˡ of the ˡ nations:
he shall take note where ˡ every ˡ man was ˡ born.

6 And the singers and the ˡ dancers · toˡgether:
shall ˡ make their ˡ song · to your ˡ name.

88

1 O Lord my God I call for ǀ help by ǀ day:
and by night also I ǀ cry ǀ out beǀfore you.

2 Let my prayer come ǀ into · your ǀ presence:
and turn your ǀ ear · to my ǀ loud ǀ crying.

†3 For my soul is ǀ filled with ǀ trouble:
and my life has come ǀ even · to the ǀ brink · of the grave.

4 I am reckoned among those that go ǀ down · to the ǀ Pit
I am a ǀ man that ǀ has no ǀ help.

5 I lie among the dead
like the slain that ǀ sleep · in the ǀ grave:
whom you remember no more
who are cut ǀ off ǀ from your ǀ power.

6 You have laid me in the ǀ lowest ǀ Pit:
in darkness and ǀ in the ǀ water·y ǀ depths.

7 Your wrath lies ǀ heavy · upǀon me:
and all your ǀ waves are ǀ brought aǀgainst me.

8 You have put my ǀ friends far ǀ from me:
and made me to ǀ be abǀhorred ǀ by them.

9 I am so fast in prison I ǀ cannot · get ǀ free:
my eyes fail beǀcause of ǀ my afǀfliction.

10 Lord I call to you ǀ every ǀ day:
I stretch ǀ out my ǀ hands toǀward you.

11 Will you work ǀ wonders · for the ǀ dead:
or will the shades rise ǀ up aǀgain to ǀ praise you?

12 Shall your love be de|clared · in the | grave:
or your faithfulness | in the | place · of de|struction?

13 Will your wonders be made | known · in the | dark:
or your righteousness‿
in the land where | all things | are for|gotten?

14 But to you Lord | will I | cry:
early in the morning my | prayer shall | come be|fore you.

15 O Lord why have | you re|jected me:
why do you | hide your | face | from me?

16 I have been afflicted and wearied from my | youth | upward:
I am tossed high and | low I | cease to | be.

17 Your fierce anger has | over|whelmed me:
and your | terrors · have | put me · to | silence.

18 They surround me like a flood | all the · day | long:
they close up|on me · from | every | side.

19 Friend and acquaintance you have put | far | from me:
and kept my com|panions | from my | sight.

89

1 Lord I will sing for ever of your | loving-|kindnesses:
my mouth shall proclaim your faithfulness‿
through|out all | gener|ations.

2 I have said of your loving-kindness‿
that it is | built for | ever:
you have established your | faithful·ness | in the heavens.

3 The Lord said 'I have made a covenant | with my chosen:
I have sworn an | oath · to my | servant | David.

4 'I will establish your | line for | ever:
and build up your | throne for | all · gener|ations.'

5 Let the heavens praise your | wonders · O | Lord:
and let your faithfulness be sung‿
in the as|sembly | of the | holy ones.

6 For who amidst the clouds can be com|pared · to the Lord:
or who is like the Lord a|mong the | sons of | heaven?

7 A God to be feared in the council | of the | holy ones:
great and terrible above | all that | are a|round him.

8 O Lord God of hosts | who is | like you?:
your power and your | faithfulness · are | all a|bout you.

9 You rule the | raging · of the | sea:
when its | waves | surge you | still them.

10 You crushed Rahab ˈ like a ˈ carcase:
you scattered your enemies ˈ by your ˈ mighty ˈ arm.

11 The heavens are yours * so also ˈ is the ˈ earth:
you founded the ˈ world and ˈ all · that is ˈ in it.

12 You created the ˈ north · and the ˈ south:
Tabor and Mount ˈ Hermon · shall ˈ sing of · your ˈ name.

13 Mighty ˈ is your ˈ arm:
strong is your hand * and your right ˈ hand is ˈ lifted ˈ high.

14 Righteousness and justice are the foundation ˈ of your ˈ throne:
loving-kindness and ˈ faithfulness · atˈtend your ˈ presence.

15 Happy the people who know the triˈumphal ˈ shout:
who walk O ˈ Lord · in the ˈ light of · your ˈ countenance.

16 They rejoice all the day long beˈcause of · your ˈ name:
because of your ˈ righteousness · they ˈ are exˈalted.

17 For you are their glory ˈ and their ˈ strength:
and our heads are upˈlifted ˈ by your ˈ favour.

18 Our king beˈlongs · to the ˈ Lord:
he that rules over us to the ˈ Holy ˈ One of ˈ Israel.

19 You spoke ˈ once · in a ˈ vision:
and ˈ said ˈ to your ˈ faithful one,

20 'I have set a youth aˈbove a ˈ warrior:
I have exalted a ˈ young man ˈ out of · the ˈ people.

21 ‘I have found my | servant | David:
and anointed him | with my | holy | oil.

22 ‘My hand | shall up|hold him:
and my | arm | shall | strengthen him.

23 ‘No enemy | shall de|ceive him:
no | evil | man shall | hurt him.

24 ‘I will crush his | adversaries · be|fore him:
and | strike down | those that | hate him.

25 ‘My faithfulness and loving-kindness | shall be | with him:
and through my name his | head · shall be | lifted | high.

26 ‘I will set the hand of his dominion‿
upon the | Western | Sea:
and his right hand shall stretch‿
to the | streams of | Meso·po|tamia.

27 ‘He will call to me | “You · are my | Father:
my God and the | Rock of | my sal|vation.”

28 ‘I will make him my | first-born | son:
and highest a|mong the | kings · of the | earth.

29 ‘I will ever maintain my loving-|kindness · to|ward him:
and my covenant | with him · shall | stand | firm.

30 ‘I will establish his | line for | ever:
and his | throne · like the | days of | heaven.

31 ‘If his children for|sake my | law:
and | will not | walk in · my | judgements;

32 ‘If they pro|fane my | statutes:
and | do not | keep · my com|mandments,

33 'Then I will punish their re¦bellion · with the ¦ rod:
and ¦ their in¦iquity · with ¦ blows.

34 'But I will not cause my loving-¦kindness · to ¦ cease‿from him:
nor‿will ¦ I be¦tray my ¦ faithfulness.

35 'I will not pro¦fane my ¦ covenant:
or alter ¦ what has ¦ passed from · my ¦ lips.

36 'Once and for all I have ¦ sworn · by my ¦ holiness:
I will ¦ not prove ¦ false to ¦ David.

37 'His posterity shall en¦dure for ¦ ever:
and his throne be ¦ as the ¦ sun be¦fore me;

38 'Like the moon that is es¦tablished · for ¦ ever:
and stands in the ¦ heavens · for ¦ ever¦more.'

39 Yet you have been enraged a¦gainst · your an¦ointed:
you have ab¦horred him ¦ and re¦jected him.

40 You have spurned the covenant ¦ with your ¦ servant:
and de¦filed his ¦ crown · to the ¦ dust.

41 You have broken down ¦ all his ¦ walls:
and ¦ made his ¦ strongholds ¦ desolate.

42 All that pass ¦ by ¦ plunder him:
he has be¦come the ¦ scorn of · his ¦ neighbours.

43 You have exalted the right hand ¦ of his ¦ adversaries:
and ¦ gladdened ¦ all his ¦ enemies.

44 His bright sword you have ¦ turned ¦ backward:
you have not en¦abled him · to ¦ stand · in the ¦ battle.

45 You have brought his ¦ lustre · to an ¦ end:
you have ¦ cast his ¦ throne · to the ¦ ground.

46 You have cut short the ' days of · his ' youth:
and ' clothed him ' with dis'honour.

47 How long O Lord will you hide your'self so ' utterly:
how long shall your ' fury ' burn like ' fire?

48 Remember how I draw to my e'ternal ' end:
have you created ' all man'kind for ' nothing?

49 Where is the man who can live and ' not see ' death:
who can deliver his ' life · from the ' power · of the '
grave?

50 Where O Lord are your loving-'kindnesses · of ' old:
which you have vowed to ' David ' in your ' faithfulness?

51 Remember O Lord how your servant ' is re'viled:
how I bear in my bosom the ' onslaught ' of the '
peoples;

52 Remember how your ' ene·mies ' taunt:
how they mock the ' footsteps · of ' your an'ointed.

(†)(53 Blessèd be the ' Lord for ' ever:
A'men and ' A–'men.)

90

1 Lord you have ˡ been our ˡ refuge:
from one generˡation ˡ to anˡother.

2 Before the mountains were born
or the earth and the world were ˡ brought to ˡ be:
from eternity to eˡterni·ty ˡ you are ˡ God.

3 You turn manˡ back · into ˡ dust:
saying 'Return to ˡ dust you ˡ sons of ˡ Adam.'

4 For a thousand years in your sight‿
are like ˡ yester·day ˡ passing:
or ˡ like one ˡ watch · of the ˡ night.

5 You cut them ˡ short · like a ˡ dream:
like the fresh ˡ grass ˡ of the ˡ morning;

6 In the morning it is ˡ green and ˡ flourishes:
at evening it is ˡ withered · and ˡ dried ˡ up.

7 And we are conˡsumed · by your ˡ anger:
because of your indigˡnation · we ˡ cease to ˡ be.

8 You have brought our inˡiquities · beˡfore you:
and our secret ˡ sins · to the ˡ light of · your ˡ countenance.

9 Our days decline beˡneath your ˡ wrath:
and our years ˡ pass aˡway · like a ˡ sigh.

10 The days of our life are three score years and ten
or if we have ˡ strength four ˡ score:
the pride of our labours is but toil and sorrow
for it passes quickly aˡway and ˡ we are ˡ gone.

11 Who can know the ǀ power of · your ǀ wrath:
who can know your indigǀnation · like ǀ those that ǀ
fear you?

12 Teach us so to ǀ number · our ǀ days:
that we may apǀply our ǀ hearts to ǀ wisdom.

13 Relent O Lord * how long will ǀ you be ǀ angry?:
take ǀ pity ǀ on your ǀ servants.

14 O satisfy us early ǀ with your ǀ mercy:
that all our days we ǀ may reǀjoice and ǀ sing.

15 Give us joy for all the days you ǀ have afǀflicted us:
for the ǀ years · we have ǀ suffered · adǀversity.

16 Show your ǀ servants · your ǀ work:
and let their ǀ children ǀ see your ǀ glory.

†17 May the gracious favour of the Lord our ǀ God · be‿
upǀon us:
prosper the work of our hands
O ǀ prosper · the ǀ work · of our ǀ hands!

91

1 He who dwells in the shelter of the ǀ Most ǀ High:
who abides under the ǀ shadow ǀ of the · Alǀmighty

2 He will say to the Lord
'You are my refuge ǀ and my ǀ stronghold:
my ǀ God in ǀ whom I ǀ trust.'

3 For he will deliver you from the | snare · of the | hunter:
and | from the · de|stroying | curse.

4 He will cover you with his wings
and you will be safe | under · his | feathers:
his faithfulness will | be your | shield · and de|fence.

5 You shall not be afraid of any | terror · by | night:
or of the | arrow · that | flies by | day,

6 Of the pestilence that walks a|bout in | darkness:
or the | plague · that de|stroys at | noonday.

7 A thousand may fall beside you
and ten thousand at your | right | hand:
but | you it | shall not | touch;

8 Your own | eyes shall | see:
and look on the re|ward | of the · un|godly.

9 The Lord him|self · is your | refuge:
you have | made the · Most | High your | stronghold.

10 Therefore no | harm · will be|fall you:
nor will any | scourge come | near your | tent.

11 For he will com|mand his | angels:
to | keep you · in | all your | ways.

12 They will bear you | up · in their | hands:
lest you dash your | foot a|gainst a | stone.

13 You will tread on the | lion · and the | adder:
the young lion and the serpent‿
you will | trample | under | foot.

14 'He has set his love upon me
and therefore I | will de|liver him:
I will lift him out of danger be|cause · he has | known
my | name.

15 'When he calls upon me ˡ I will ˡ answer him:
I will be with him in trouble
I will ˡ rescue him · and ˡ bring him · to ˡ honour.

16 'With long ˡ life · I will ˡ satisfy him:
and ˡ fill him · with ˡ my salˡvation.'

92

1 How good to give ˡ thanks · to the ˡ Lord:
to sing praises to your ˡ name ˡ O Most ˡ High,

2 To declare your ˡ love · in the ˡ morning:
and at ˡ night to ˡ sing of · your ˡ faithfulness,

†3 Upon the lute upon the lute of ˡ ten ˡ strings:
and to the ˡ melo·dy ˡ of the ˡ lyre.

4 For in all you have done O Lord you have ˡ made me ˡ glad:
I will sing for joy beˡcause of · the ˡ works · of your ˡ hands.

5 Lord how glorious ˡ are your ˡ works:
your ˡ thoughts are ˡ very ˡ deep.

6 The brutish do ˡ not conˡsider:
and the ˡ fool · cannot ˡ underˡstand

7 That though the wicked ˡ sprout like ˡ grass:
and ˡ all wrongˡdoers ˡ flourish,

8 They flourish to be deˡstroyed · for ˡ ever:
but you Lord are exˡalted · for ˡ everˡmore.

9 For behold your enemies O Lord‿
your ǀ enemies · shall ǀ perish:
and all the workers of ǀ wicked·ness ǀ shall be ǀ scattered.

10 You have lifted up my head
like the horns of the ǀ wild ǀ oxen:
I am anǀointed · with ǀ fresh ǀ oil;

11 My eyes have looked ǀ down · on my ǀ enemies:
and my ears have heard the ruin‿
of ǀ those who · rose ǀ up aǀgainst me.

12 The righteous shall ǀ flourish · like the ǀ palm tree:
they shall spread aǀbroad · like a ǀ cedar · in ǀ Lebanon;

13 For they are planted in the ǀ house · of the ǀ Lord:
and flourish in the ǀ courts of ǀ our ǀ God.

14 In old age they shall be ǀ full of ǀ sap:
they shall be ǀ sturdy · and ǀ laden · with ǀ branches;

15 And they will say that the ǀ Lord is ǀ just:
the Lord my Rock in ǀ whom is ǀ no unǀrighteousness.

93

1 The Lord is King * and has put on ǀ robes of ǀ glory:
the Lord has put on his glory
he has ǀ girded · himǀself with ǀ strength.

2 He has made the ǀ world so ǀ firm:
that it ǀ cannot ǀ be ǀ moved.

3 Your throne is esǀtablished · from of ǀ old:
you ǀ are from ǀ everǀlasting.

4 The floods have lifted up O Lord
the floods have lifted | up their | voice:
the | floods lift | up their | pounding.

5 But mightier than the sound of many waters
than the mighty waters or the | breakers · of the | sea:
the | Lord on | high is | mighty.

6 Your decrees are | very | sure:
and holiness O Lord a|dorns your | house for | ever.

94

1 O Lord God to whom | vengeance · be|longs:
O God to whom vengeance be|longs shine | out in | glory.

2 Arise | judge · of the | earth:
and requite the | proud as | they de|serve.

3 Lord how | long · shall the | wicked:
how | long · shall the | wicked | triumph?

4 How long shall all evildoers | pour out | words:
how | long · shall they | boast and | flaunt themselves?

5 They crush your | people · O | Lord:
they op|press your | own pos|session.

6 They murder the | widow · and the | alien:
they | put the | fatherless · to | death.

7 And they say 'The | Lord · does not | see:
nor does the | God of | Jacob · con|sider it.'

8 Consider this you senseless a¦mong the ¦ people:
fools ¦ when · will you ¦ under¦stand?

9 He who planted the ear does ¦ he not ¦ hear:
he who formed the ¦ eye does ¦ he not ¦ see?

10 He who disciplines the nations will ¦ he not ¦ punish:
has the ¦ teacher · of man¦kind no ¦ knowledge?

†11 The Lord knows the ¦ thoughts of ¦ man:
he ¦ knows · that they ¦ are mere ¦ breath.

12 Blessèd is the man whom you ¦ discipline · O ¦ Lord:
and ¦ teach ¦ from your ¦ law,

13 Giving him rest from ¦ days of ¦ misery:
till a ¦ pit is ¦ dug · for the ¦ wicked.

14 The Lord will not cast ¦ off his ¦ people:
nor ¦ will he · for¦sake his ¦ own.

15 For justice shall return to the ¦ righteous ¦ man:
and with him to ¦ all the ¦ true of ¦ heart.

16 Who will stand up for me a¦gainst the ¦ wicked:
who will take my part a¦gainst the ¦ evil¦doers?

17 If the Lord had not ¦ been my ¦ helper:
I would soon have ¦ dwelt · in the ¦ land of ¦ silence.

18 But when I said 'My ¦ foot has ¦ slipped':
your ¦ mercy · O ¦ Lord was ¦ holding me.

19 In all the ¦ doubts · of my ¦ heart:
your consol¦ations · de¦lighted · my ¦ soul.

20 Will you be any friend to the ¦ court of ¦ wickedness:
that contrives ¦ evil · by ¦ means of ¦ law?

21 They band together against the | life · of the | righteous:
and con|demn | inno·cent | blood.

22 But the | Lord · is my | stronghold:
my | God · is my | rock · and my | refuge.

23 Let him requite them for their wickedness
and silence them | for their | evil:
the | Lord our | God shall | silence them.

95

1 O come let us sing | out · to the | Lord:
let us shout in triumph to the | rock of | our sal|vation

2 Let us come before his | face with | thanksgiving:
and cry | out to · him | joyfully · in | psalms.

3 For the Lord is a | great | God:
and a great | king a·bove | all | gods.

4 In his hand are the | depths · of the | earth:
and the peaks of the | mountains · are | his | also.

†5 The sea is his and | he | made it:
his hands | moulded | dry | land.

6 Come let us worship and | bow | down:
and kneel be|fore the | Lord our | maker.

7 For he is the | Lord our | God:
we are his | people · and the | sheep of · his | pasture

8 Today if only you would hear his voice
'Do not harden your | hearts · as at | Meribah:
as on that day at | Massah | in the | wilderness;

9 'When your | fathers | tested me:
put me to proof though | they had | seen my | works.

10 'Forty years long I loathed that gener|ation · and | said:
"It is a people who err in their hearts
for they | do not | know my | ways";

11 'Of whom I | swore · in my | wrath:
"They | shall not | enter · my | rest."'

96

1 O sing to the Lord a | new | song:
sing to the | Lord | all the | earth.

2 Sing to the Lord and bless his | holy | name:
proclaim the good news of his sal|vation · from | day
to | day.

3 Declare his glory a|mong the | nations:
and his | wonders · a|mong all | peoples.

4 For great is the Lord and | greatly · to be | praised:
he is more to be | feared than | all | gods.

5 As for all the gods of the nations | they are · mere |
idols:
it is the | Lord who | made the | heavens.

6 Majesty and | glory · are be|fore him:
beauty and | power are | in his | sanctuary.

7 Render to the Lord you families | of the | nations:
render to the | Lord | glory · and | might.

8 Render to the Lord the honour | due · to his | name
bring offerings and | come in|to his | courts.

9 O worship the Lord in the beauty | of his | holiness:
let the whole earth | stand in | awe of | him.

10 Say among the nations that the | Lord is | king:
he has made the world so firm that it can never b
moved
and he shall | judge the | peoples · with | equity.

11 Let the heavens rejoice and let the | earth be | glad:
let the sea | roar and | all that | fills it;

12 Let the fields rejoice and | every·thing | in them:
then shall all the trees of the wood‿
shout with | joy be|fore the | Lord;

†13 For he comes he comes to | judge the | earth:
he shall judge the world with righteousness
and the | peoples | with his | truth.

97

1 The Lord is king let the | earth re|joice:
let the | multitude · of | islands · be | glad.

2 Clouds and darkness are | round a|bout him:
righteousness and justice are the found|ation | of his |
throne.

3 Fire | goes be|fore him:
and burns up his | enemies · on | every | side.

4 His lightnings ǀ light the ǀ world:
the ǀ earth ǀ sees it · and ǀ quakes.

5 The mountains melt like wax beǀfore his ǀ face:
from before the face of the ǀ Lord of ǀ all the ǀ earth.

6 The heavens have proǀclaimed his ǀ righteousness:
and all ǀ peoples · have ǀ seen his ǀ glory.

7 They are ashamed * all those who serve idols‿
and glory in ǀ mere ǀ nothings:
all ǀ gods bow ǀ down beǀfore him.

8 Zion heard and was glad * and the daughters of ǀ
Judah · reǀjoiced:
beǀcause of · your ǀ judgements · O ǀ God.

9 For you Lord are most high over ǀ all the ǀ earth:
you are exalted ǀ far a·bove ǀ all ǀ gods.

10 The Lord loves ǀ those that · hate ǀ evil:
the Lord guards the life of the faithful
and delivers them from the ǀ hand of ǀ the unǀgodly.

11 Light ǀ dawns · for the ǀ righteous:
and ǀ joy · for the ǀ true of ǀ heart.

12 Rejoice in the ǀ Lord you ǀ righteous:
and give ǀ thanks · to his ǀ holy ǀ name.

98

1 O sing to the Lord a | new | song:
for he has | done | marvel·lous | things;

2 His right hand and his | holy | arm:
they have | got | him the | victory.

3 The Lord has made | known · his sal|vation:
he has revealed his just de|liverance · in the | sight of · the | nations.

4 He has remembered his mercy and faithfulness‿ towards the | house of | Israel:
and all the ends of the earth‿ have seen the sal|vation | of our | God.

5 Shout with joy to the Lord | all the | earth:
break into | singing · and | make | melody.

6 Make melody to the Lord up|on the | harp:
upon the harp and | with the | sounds of | praise.

7 With trumpets | and with | horns:
cry out in triumph be|fore the | Lord the | king.

8 Let the sea roar and | all that | fills it:
the good earth and | those who | live up|on it.

9 Let the rivers | clap their | hands:
and let the mountains ring out to|gether · be|fore the | Lord;

10 For he comes to | judge the | earth:
he shall judge the world with righteousness and the | peoples | with | equity.

99

1 The Lord is king let the | nations | tremble:
he is enthroned upon the cherubim | let the | earth |
quake.

2 The Lord is | great in | Zion:
he is | high a|bove all | nations.

3 Let them praise your great and | terri·ble | name:
for | holy | is the | Lord.

4 The Mighty One is king and | loves | justice:
you have established equity * you have dealt |‿
righteousness · and | justice · in | Jacob.

†5 *O exalt the | Lord our | God:*
and bow down before his | footstool · for | he is | holy.

6 Moses and Aaron among his priests
and Samuel among those who call up|on his | name:
they called to the | Lord | and he | answered.

7 He spoke to them from the | pillar · of | cloud:
they kept to his teachings | and the | law · that he |
gave them.

8 You answered them O | Lord our | God:
you were a forgiving God to them
and | pardoned · their | wrong|doing.

9 *O exalt the | Lord our | God:*
and bow down towards his holy hill
for the | Lord our | God is | holy.

100

1 O shout to the Lord in triumph | all the | earth:
serve the Lord with gladness
and come before his | face with | songs of | joy.

2 Know that the Lord | he is | God:
it is he who has made us and we are his
we are his | people · and the | sheep of · his | pasture

3 Come into his gates with thanksgiving
and into his | courts with | praise:
give thanks to him and | bless his | holy | name.

4 For the Lord is good * his loving mercy | is for | ever:
his faithfulness through|out all | gener|ations.

101

1 My song shall be of | steadfastness · and | justice:
to | you Lord | will I | sing.

2 I will be wise in the | way of | innocence:
O | when | will you | come to me?

3 I will walk with|in my | house:
in| puri|ty of | heart.

4 I will set nothing evil be|fore my | eyes:
I hate the sin of backsliders it shall | get no | hold |
on me.

†5 Crookedness of heart shall de|part | from me:
I will | know | nothing · of | wickedness.

[6 The man who secretly slanders his neighbour I | will de|stroy:
the proud look and the arrogant | heart · I will | not en|dure.]

7 My eyes shall look to the faithful in the land
and they shall | make their | home with me:
one who walks in the way of innocence |‿
he shall | minis·ter | to me.

8 No man who practises deceit shall | live in · my | house:
no one who utters | lies shall | stand in · my | sight.

[9 Morning by morning I will destroy‿
all the | wicked · of the | land:
and cut off all evildoers‿
from the | city | of the | Lord.]

102

1 O Lord | hear my | prayer:
and | let my | cry | come to you.

2 Do not hide your face from me in the | day of · my | trouble:
turn your ear to me
and when I | call be | swift to | answer.

3 For my days pass a|way like | smoke:
and my bones | burn as | in a | furnace.

4 My heart is scorched and ˈ withered · like ˈ grass:
and I forˈget to ˈ eat my ˈ bread.

5 I am weary with the ˈ sound of · my ˈ groaning:
my ˈ bones stick ˈ fast to · my ˈ skin.

6 I have become like an ˈ owl · in the ˈ wilderness:
like a ˈ screech-owl · aˈmong the ˈ ruins.

7 I keep watch and ˈ flit · to and ˈ fro:
like a ˈ sparrow · upˈon a ˈ housetop.

8 My enemies taunt me ˈ all day ˈ long:
and those who ˈ rave at me · make ˈ oaths aˈgainst me.

9 Surely I have eaten ˈ ashes · for ˈ bread:
and ˈ mingled · my ˈ drink with ˈ tears,

10 Because of your wrath and ˈ indigˈnation:
for you have taken me ˈ up and ˈ tossed · me aˈside.

†11 My days deˈcline · like a ˈ shadow:
and I ˈ wither · aˈway like ˈ grass.

12 But you Lord are enˈthroned for ˈ ever:
and your name shall be known throughˈout all ˈ generˈations.

13 You will arise and have ˈ mercy up·on ˈ Zion:
for it is time to pity her the apˈpointed ˈ time has ˈ come.

14 Your servants love ˈ even · her ˈ stones:
and her ˈ dust moves ˈ them to ˈ pity.

15 Then shall the nations fear your ˈ name O ˈ Lord:
and all the ˈ kings · of the ˈ earth your ˈ glory,

16 When the Lord has ꞁ built up ꞁ Zion:
when he ꞁ shows himꞁself · in his ꞁ glory,

17 When he turns to the ꞁ prayer · of the ꞁ destitute:
and does not deꞁspise their ꞁ suppliꞁcation.

†18 Let this be written down for ꞁ those who · come ꞁ after:
and a people yet unꞁborn will ꞁ praise the ꞁ Lord.

19 For the Lord has looked down from the ꞁ height · of his ꞁ holiness:
from heaven he has ꞁ looked upꞁon the ꞁ earth,

20 To hear the ꞁ groaning · of the ꞁ prisoner:
to deliver ꞁ those conꞁdemned to ꞁ die;

21 That they may proclaim the name of the ꞁ Lord in ꞁ Zion:
and his ꞁ praises ꞁ in Jeꞁrusalem,

22 When the nations are ꞁ gathered · toꞁgether:
and the ꞁ kingdoms · to ꞁ serve the ꞁ Lord.

23 He has broken my strength beꞁfore my ꞁ time:
he has ꞁ cut ꞁ short my ꞁ days.

24 Do not take me away O God in the ꞁ midst of · my ꞁ life:
you whose years exꞁtend through ꞁ all · generꞁations.

25 In the beginning you laid the founꞁdations · of the ꞁ earth:
and the ꞁ heavens · are the ꞁ work of · your ꞁ hands.

26 They shall perish but ꞁ you · will enꞁdure:
they shall all grow old like a garment
like clothes you will change them and ꞁ they shall ꞁ pass aꞁway.

27 But you are the ǀ same for ǀ ever:
and your ǀ years will ǀ never ǀ fail.

28 The children of your servants shall ǀ rest seǀcure:
and their seed shall be esǀtablished ǀ in your ǀ sight

103

1 Praise the Lord ǀ O my ǀ soul:
and all that is within me ǀ praise his ǀ holy ǀ name.

2 Praise the Lord ǀ O my ǀ soul:
and forǀget not ǀ all his ǀ benefits,

3 Who forgives ǀ all your ǀ sin:
and ǀ heals ǀ all · your inǀfirmities,

4 Who redeems your ǀ life · from the ǀ Pit:
and crowns you with ǀ mercy ǀ and comǀpassion;

†5 Who satisfies your being with ǀ good ǀ things:
so that your ǀ youth · is reǀnewed · like an ǀ eagle's.

6 The Lord ǀ works ǀ righteousness:
and justice for ǀ all who ǀ are opǀpressed.

7 He made known his ǀ ways to ǀ Moses:
and his ǀ works · to the ǀ children · of ǀ Israel.

8 The Lord is full of comǀpassion · and ǀ mercy:
slow to anger ǀ and of ǀ great ǀ goodness.

9 He will not ǀ always · be ǀ chiding:
nor will he ǀ keep his ǀ anger · for ǀ ever.

10 He has not dealt with us ac¦cording · to our ¦ sins:
nor rewarded us ac¦cording ¦ to our ¦ wickedness.

11 For as the heavens are high a¦bove the ¦ earth:
so great is his ¦ mercy · over ¦ those that ¦ fear him;

12 As far as the east is ¦ from the ¦ west:
so far has he ¦ set our ¦ sins ¦ from us.

13 As a father is tender to¦wards his ¦ children:
so is the Lord ¦ tender · to ¦ those that ¦ fear him.

†14 For he knows of ¦ what · we are ¦ made:
he re¦members · that we ¦ are but ¦ dust.

15 The days of man are ¦ but as ¦ grass:
he flourishes ¦ like a ¦ flower · of the ¦ field;

16 When the wind goes over it ¦ it is ¦ gone:
and its ¦ place will ¦ know it · no ¦ more.

17 But the merciful goodness of the Lord
endures for ever and ever toward ¦ ‿
those that ¦ fear him:
and his righteousness up¦on their ¦ ‿
children's ¦ children;

18 Upon those who ¦ keep his ¦ covenant:
and ¦ remember · his com¦mandments · to ¦ do them.

19 The Lord has established his ¦ throne in ¦ heaven:
and his ¦ kingdom ¦ rules · over ¦ all.

20 Praise the Lord all you his angels
you that ex¦cel in ¦ strength:
you that fulfil his word
and obey the ¦ voice of ¦ his com¦mandment.

21 Praise the Lord all ꞁ you his ꞁ hosts:
his ꞁ servants · who ꞁ do his ꞁ will.

22 Praise the Lord all his works
in all places of ꞁ his doꞁminion:
praise the ꞁ Lord ꞁ O my ꞁ soul!

104

1 Bless the Lord ꞁ O my ꞁ soul:
O Lord my ꞁ God how ꞁ great you ꞁ are!

2 Clothed with ꞁ majesty · and ꞁ honour:
wrapped in ꞁ light as ꞁ in a ꞁ garment.

3 You have stretched out the ꞁ heavens · like a ꞁ tent-cloth:
and laid the beams of your ꞁ dwelling · upꞁon their ꞁ
waters;

4 You make the ꞁ clouds your ꞁ chariot:
and ꞁ ride up · on the ꞁ wings · of the ꞁ wind;

5 You make the ꞁ winds your ꞁ messengers:
and ꞁ flames of ꞁ fire your ꞁ ministers;

6 You have set the earth on ꞁ its foundꞁations:
so ꞁ that it · shall ꞁ never · be ꞁ moved.

7 The deep covered it ꞁ as · with a ꞁ mantle:
the waters ꞁ stood aꞁbove the ꞁ hills.

8 At your reꞁbuke they ꞁ fled:
at the voice of your ꞁ thunder · they ꞁ hurried · aꞁway;

9 They went up to the mountains
they went | down · by the | valleys:
to the place which | you · had ap|pointed | for them.

10 You fixed a limit which they | may not | pass:
they shall not return a|gain to | cover · the | earth.

11 You send springs | into · the | gullies:
which | run be|tween the | hills;

12 They give drink to every | beast · of the | field:
and the wild | asses | quench their | thirst.

13 Beside them the birds of the air | build their | nests:
and | sing a|mong the | branches.

14 You water the mountains from your | dwelling · on | high:
and the earth is | filled · by the | fruits of · your | work.

15 You cause the grass to | grow · for the | cattle:
and all green things for the | servants | of man|kind.

16 You bring food | out of · the | earth:
and wine that makes | glad the | heart of | man,

17 Oil to give him a | shining | countenance:
and | bread to | strengthen · his | heart.

18 The trees of the Lord are | well-|watered:
the cedars of | Lebanon · that | he has | planted,

19 Where the birds | build their | nests:
and the stork | makes her | home · in the | pine-tops.

20 The high hills are a refuge for the | wild | goats:
and the crags a | cover | for the | conies.

21 You created the moon to | mark the | seasons:
and the sun | knows the | hour · of its | setting.

22 You make darkness ¦ and it · is ¦ night:
in which all the beasts of the ¦ forest ¦ move by ¦ stealth.

23 The lions ¦ roar · for their ¦ prey:
seek¦ing their ¦ food from ¦ God.

24 When the sun rises ¦ they re¦tire:
and ¦ lay them·selves ¦ down · in their ¦ dens.

†25 Man goes ¦ out · to his ¦ work:
and to his ¦ labour · un¦til the ¦ evening.

26 Lord how various ¦ are your ¦ works:
in wisdom you have made them all
and the ¦ earth is ¦ full of · your ¦ creatures.

27 There is the wide im¦measur·able ¦ sea:
there move living things without ¦ number ¦ great and ¦ small;

28 There go the ships ¦ to and ¦ fro:
and there is that Leviathan
whom you ¦ formed to ¦ sport · in the ¦ deep.

29 These all ¦ look to ¦ you:
to give them their ¦ food in ¦ due ¦ season.

30 When you give it to ¦ them they ¦ gather it:
when you open your hand they are ¦ satisfied · with ¦ good ¦ things.

31 When you hide your ¦ face · they are ¦ troubled:
when you take away their breath‿
they ¦ die · and re¦turn · to their ¦ dust.

†32 When you send forth your spirit they ¦ are cre¦ated:
and you re¦new the ¦ face · of the ¦ earth.

33 May the glory of the Lord en¦dure for ¦ ever:
may the ¦ Lord re¦joice · in his ¦ works.

34 If he look upon the ¦ earth · it shall ¦ tremble:
if he but touch the ¦ mountains ¦ they shall ¦ smoke.

35 I will sing to the Lord as ¦ long as · I ¦ live:
I will praise my ¦ God · while I ¦ have · any ¦ being.

36 May my meditation be ¦ pleasing ¦ to him:
for my ¦ joy shall ¦ be · in the ¦ Lord.

†37 May sinners perish from the earth
let the wicked ¦ be no ¦ more:
bless the Lord O my soul
O ¦ praise ¦ – the ¦ Lord.

105

1 O give thanks to the Lord and call up¦on his ¦ name:
tell among the ¦ peoples · what ¦ things · he has ¦ done.

2 Sing to him O ¦ sing ¦ praises:
and be telling of ¦ all his ¦ marvel·lous ¦ works.

3 Exult in his ¦ holy ¦ name:
and let those that seek the ¦ Lord be ¦ joyful · in ¦ heart.

4 Seek the ¦ Lord · and his ¦ strength:
O ¦ seek his ¦ face con¦tinually.

5 Call to mind what wonders ¦ he has ¦ done:
his marvellous acts and the ¦ judgements ¦ of his ¦ mouth,

6 O seed of ǀ Abraham · his ǀ servant:
O ǀ children · of ǀ Jacob · his ǀ chosen one.

7 For he is the ǀ Lord our ǀ God:
and his judgements ǀ are in ǀ all the ǀ earth.

8 He has remembered his ǀ covenant · for ǀ ever:
the word that he ordained for a ǀ thousand ǀ
gener ǀ ations,

9 The covenant that he ǀ made with ǀ Abraham:
the ǀ oath · that he ǀ swore to ǀ Isaac,

10 And confirmed it to ǀ Jacob · as a ǀ statute:
to Israel as an ǀ ever ǀ lasting ǀ covenant,

11 Saying 'I will give you the ǀ land of ǀ Canaan:
to be the ǀ portion · of ǀ your in ǀ heritance',

12 And that when they ǀ were but ǀ few:
little in number and ǀ ali·ens ǀ in the ǀ land.

13 They wandered from ǀ nation · to ǀ nation:
from one people and ǀ kingdom ǀ to an ǀ other.

14 He suffered no man to ǀ do them ǀ wrong:
but re ǀ proved · even ǀ kings for · their ǀ sake,

†15 Saying 'Touch not ǀ my an ǀ ointed:
and ǀ do my ǀ prophets · no ǀ harm.'

16 Then he called down a ǀ famine · on the ǀ land:
and destroyed the ǀ bread that ǀ was their ǀ stay.

17 But he had sent a ǀ man a ǀ head of them:
Joseph ǀ who was ǀ sold · into ǀ slavery,

18 Whose feet they | fastened · with | fetters:
and thrust his | neck in·to a | hoop of | iron.

19 Till the time that his | words proved | true:
he was | tested · by the | Lord's com|mand.

20 Then the king | sent and | loosed him:
the ruler of | nations | set him | free;

21 He made him master | of his | household:
and ruler | over | all · his pos|sessions,

†22 To rebuke his | officers · at | will:
and to | teach his | counsel·lors | wisdom.

23 Then Israel | came · into | Egypt:
and Jacob | dwelt · in the | land of | Ham.

24 There the Lord made his | people | fruitful:
too | numer·ous | for their | enemies,

25 Whose hearts he turned to | hate his | people:
and to deal de|ceitful·ly | with his | servants.

26 Then he sent | Moses · his | servant:
and | Aaron · whom | he had | chosen.

27 Through them he | manifested · his | signs:
and his | wonders · in the | land of | Ham.

28 He sent darkness | and it · was | dark:
yet they would | not o|bey · his com|mands.

29 He turned their | waters · into | blood:
and | slew the | fish there|in.

30 Their country | swarmed with | frogs:
even the inner | chambers | of their | kings.

31 He spoke the word and there came great | swarms of | flies:
and | gnats with·in | all their | borders.

32 He sent them | storms of | hail:
and darts of | fire | into · their | land.

33 He struck their | vines · and their | fig-trees:
and shattered the | trees with|in their | borders.

34 He commanded and there | came | grasshoppers:
and young | locusts · with|out | number.

35 They ate up every green thing | in the | land:
and de|voured the | fruit · of the | soil.

36 He smote all the first-born | in their | land:
the | first-fruits · of | all their | manhood.

37 He brought Israel out with silver | and with | gold:
and not one among their | tribes was | seen to stumble.

38 Egypt was | glad · at their | going:
for dread of | Israel · had | fallen · up|on them.

39 He spread out a | cloud · for a | covering:
and | fire to | lighten · the | night.

40 The people asked and he | brought them | quails:
and satisfied them | with the | bread from | heaven.

41 He opened a rock so that the | waters | gushed:
and ran in the parched | land | like a | river.

42 For he had remembered his | holy | word:
that he gave to | Abra|ham his | servant.

43 So he led out his | people · with re|joicing:
his | chosen ones · with | shouts of | joy;

44 He gave them the | land · of the | nations:
and they took possession of the | fruit‿
of | other · men's | toil,

45 So that they might | keep his | statutes:
and faithfully obey his laws
O | praise | – the | Lord.

106

1 Praise the Lord
O give thanks to the Lord for | he is | good:
and his | mercy · en|dures for | ever.

2 Who can express the mighty | acts · of the | Lord:
or | fully | voice his | praise?

3 Blessèd are those who act ac|cording · to | justice:
who at | all times | do the | right.

4 Remember me O Lord
when you visit your people | with your | favour:
and come to me | also · with | your sal|vation,

†5 That I may see the prosperity | of your | chosen:
that I may rejoice with the rejoicing of your people
and exult with | those who | are your | own.

6 We have sinned | like our | fathers:
we have acted per|versely · and | done | wrong.

7 Our fathers when they | were in | Egypt:
took no | heed | of your | wonders;

8 They did not remember‿
the multitude of your | loving-|kindnesses:
but they re|belled · at the | Red | Sea.

9 Nevertheless he saved them for his | name's | sake:
that he | might make | known his | power.

10 He commanded the Red Sea and it | dried | up:
and he led them through the | deep as | through a
desert.

11 He delivered them from the | hand · of their | ad
versary:
and redeemed them | from the | power · of the
enemy.

12 The waters closed over | their op|pressors:
so that not | one was | left a|live.

13 Then they be|lieved his | words:
and | sang him | songs of | praise.

14 But in a little while they forgot what | he had | done
and would | wait · for his | counsel · no | more.

15 Greed took hold of them | in the | desert:
and they put | God · to the | test · in the | wilderness

16 So he gave them that which | they de|sired:
but sent a | wasting | sickness · a|mong them.

17 Then they grew envious of Moses | in the | camp:
and of Aaron the | holy · one | of the | Lord;

18 Whereupon the earth opened and | swallowed · up
Dathan:
it closed over the | compan·y | of A|biram;

19 Fire flared out a¦gainst their ¦ number:
and ¦ flame de¦voured · the un¦godly.

20 At Horeb they ¦ made themselves · a ¦ calf:
and bowed down in ¦ worship ¦ to an ¦ image.

21 And so they exchanged the ¦ glory · of ¦ God:
for the likeness of an ¦ ox that ¦ eats ¦ hay.

22 They forgot God who ¦ was their ¦ saviour:
that had done such ¦ great ¦ things in ¦ Egypt,

23 Who had worked his wonders in the ¦ land of ¦ Ham:
and his terrible ¦ deeds · at the ¦ Red ¦ Sea.

†24 Therefore he ¦ thought · to de¦stroy them:
had not Moses his servant stood before him in the breach
to turn a¦way his ¦ wrath · from de¦stroying them.

25 Then they despised the ¦ pleasant ¦ land:
and ¦ put no ¦ faith · in his ¦ promise,

26 But murmured ¦ in their ¦ tents:
and would not o¦bey the ¦ voice · of the ¦ Lord.

27 So he lifted his hand to swear an ¦ oath a¦gainst them:
that he would ¦ strike them ¦ down · in the ¦ wilderness,

28 And cast out their children a¦mong the ¦ nations:
and ¦ scatter them · through ¦ all the ¦ lands.

29 Then they joined themselves to the ¦ Baal · of ¦ Peor:
and ate things sacrificed to ¦ gods that ¦ have no ¦ life.

30 They provoked him to anger with their ¦ wanton ¦ deeds:
and ¦ plague broke ¦ out a¦mong them.

31 Then stood up Phinehas and ˈ interˈposed:
and ˈ so the ˈ plague was ˈ ended;

32 And that was counted to ˈ him for ˈ righteousness:
throughout all generˈations · for ˈ everˈmore.

33 They angered God also at the ˈ waters · of ˈ Meribah
so that Moses ˈ suffered · for ˈ their misˈdeeds;

34 For they had emˈbittered · his ˈ spirit:
and he spoke ˈ rashly ˈ with his ˈ lips.

35 They did not deˈstroy the ˈ peoples:
as the Lord had comˈmanded ˈ them to ˈ do,

36 But they mingled themselves ˈ with the ˈ heathen:
and ˈ learned to ˈ follow · their ˈ ways.

37 They worshipped ˈ foreign ˈ idols:
and ˈ these beˈcame their ˈ snare,

38 So that they ˈ sacrificed · their ˈ sons:
and their ˈ own ˈ daughters · to ˈ demons.

39 They shed ˈ inno·cent ˈ blood:
even the blood of their ˈ own ˈ sons and ˈ daughters

40 Whom they offered to the ˈ idols · of ˈ Canaan:
and the ˈ land · was deˈfiled with ˈ blood.

41 They made themselves ˈ foul · by their ˈ acts:
and with wanton deeds ˈ whored · after ˈ strange gods.

42 Then was the wrath of the Lord kindled aˈgainst his people:
and he ˈ loathed his ˈ own posˈsession;

43 He gave them into the | hands · of the | nations:
and their | adver·saries | ruled | over them.

44 Their enemies be|came · their op|pressors:
and they were brought into sub|jection · be|neath
their | power.

45 Many a | time he | saved them:
but they rebelled against him to follow their own
designs
and were brought | down | by their | wickedness.

46 Nevertheless he looked on | their dis|tress:
when he | heard their | loud | crying.

47 He remembered his | coven·ant | with them:
and relented according to the a|bundance ·
of his | loving-|kindness.

48 And he caused them | to be | pitied:
even by | those that | held them | captive.

†)49 Save us O Lord our God
and gather us from a|mong the | nations:
that we may give thanks to your holy name
and | make our | boast · in your | praises.

(50 Blessèd be the Lord the God of Israel
from everlasting to | ever|lasting:
and let all the people say Amen |
Praise | – the | Lord.)

107

1 O give thanks to the Lord for | he is | good:
for his loving | mercy | is for | ever.

2 Let the Lord's re|deemed | say so:
whom he has redeemed from the | hand | of the | enemy,

†3 And gathered in from every land
from the east and | from the | west:
from the | north and | from the | south.

4 Some went astray in the wilderness and | in the | desert:
and found no | path to · an in|habit·ed | city;

5 They were | hungry · and | thirsty:
and their | heart | fainted · with|in them.

6 Then they cried to the Lord in | their dis|tress:
and he | took them | out of · their | trouble.

7 He led them by the | right | path:
till they | came to · an in|habit·ed | city.

8 *Let them thank the | Lord · for his | goodness:*
and for the wonders that he | does · for the | children · of | men;

9 *For he | satisfies · the | thirsty:*
and fills the | hungry · with | good | things.

10 Some sat in darkness and in | deadly | shadow:
bound | fast · in af|fliction · and | iron,

11 Because they had rebelled against the | words of | God:
and scorned the purposes | of the | Most | High.

12 So he bowed down their | hearts · with af|fliction:
they tripped | headlong · with | none to | help them.

13 Then they cried to the Lord in | their dis|tress:
and he | took them | out of · their | trouble.

†14 He brought them out from darkness and | deadly | shadow:
and | broke their | chains in | two.

15 *Let them thank the | Lord · for his | goodness:*
and for the wonders that he | does · for the | children · of | men;

16 *For he shatters the | doors of | bronze:*
and | cleaves the | bars of | iron.

17 Fools were far | gone · in trans|gression:
and be|cause of · their | sins · were af|flicted.

18 They sickened at | any | food:
and had | come · to the | gates of | death.

19 Then they cried to the Lord in | their dis|tress:
and he | took them | out of · their | trouble.

20 He sent his | word and | healed them:
and | saved their | life · from the | Pit.

21 *Let them thank the | Lord · for his | goodness:*
and for the wonders that he | does · for the | children · of | men;

22 *Let them offer sacrifices of | thanks|giving:*
and tell what he has | done with | shouts of | joy.

23 Those who go down to the | sea in | ships:
and follow their | trade on | great | waters,

24 These men have seen the ˡ works of ˡ God:
and his ˡ wonders ˡ in the ˡ deep.

25 For he spoke and ˡ raised the ˡ storm-wind:
and it lifted ˡ high the ˡ waves · of the ˡ sea.

26 They go up to the sky and down aˡgain · to the ˡ depths:
their courage melts aˡway · in the ˡ face · of disˡaster

27 They reel and stagger like ˡ drunken ˡ men:
and are ˡ at their ˡ wits' ˡ end.

28 Then they cried to the Lord in ˡ their disˡtress:
and he ˡ took them ˡ out of · their ˡ trouble.

29 He calmed the ˡ storm · to a ˡ silence:
and the ˡ waves · of the ˡ sea were ˡ stilled.

30 Then they were glad beˡcause · they were ˡ quiet:
and he ˡ brought them · to the ˡ haven · they ˡ longed for.

31 *Let them thank the ˡ Lord · for his ˡ goodness:*
and for the wonders that he ˡ does · for the ˡ children · of ˡ men;

32 *Let them exalt him in the asˡsembly · of the ˡ people:*
and ˡ praise him · in the ˡ council · of ˡ elders.

33 He turns the ˡ rivers · into ˡ desert:
and springs of ˡ water · into ˡ thirsty ˡ ground.

34 He makes of a fruitful land a ˡ salty ˡ waste:
beˡcause · its inˡhabitants · are ˡ evil.

35 He turns the wilderness into a ˡ pool of ˡ water:
and parched ˡ ground · into ˡ flowing ˡ springs.

36 And there he ˡ settles · the ˡ hungry:
and they ˡ build a ˡ city · to ˡ live in.

37 They sow fields and ˡ plant ˡ vineyards:
which ˡ give them ˡ fruitful ˡ harvest.

38 He blesses them and they ˡ multi·ply ˡ greatly:
he does not ˡ let their ˡ cattle · dimˡinish.

39 But he pours conˡtempt up·on ˡ princes:
and makes them ˡ stray · in the ˡ pathless ˡ desert;

40 They are weakened and ˡ brought ˡ low:
through ˡ stress of · adˡversity · and ˡ sorrow.

41 But he lifts the ˡ poor · out of ˡ misery:
and increases their ˡ families · like ˡ flocks of ˡ sheep.

42 The upright shall ˡ see it · and reˡjoice:
and all ˡ wickedness · shall ˡ shut its ˡ mouth.

†43 Whoever is wise let him obˡserve these ˡ things:
and consider the loving-ˡkindness ˡ of the ˡ Lord.

108

1 My heart is fixed O God my ˡ heart is ˡ fixed:
I will ˡ sing and ˡ make ˡ melody.

2 Awake my soul awake ˡ lute and ˡ harp:
for ˡ I · will aˡwaken · the ˡ morning.

3 I will give you thanks O Lord aˡmong the ˡ peoples:
I will sing your ˡ praise aˡmong the ˡ nations.

4 For the greatness of your mercy ¦ reaches · to the heavens:
and your ¦ faithful·ness ¦ to the ¦ clouds.

5 Be exalted O God a¦bove the ¦ heavens:
and let your glory be ¦ over ¦ all the ¦ earth;

6 That those whom you love may ¦ be de¦livered:
O save us by ¦ your right ¦ hand and ¦ answer me.

7 God has said in his ¦ holy ¦ place:
'I will exult and divide Shechem
I will parcel ¦ out the ¦ valley · of ¦ Succoth.

8 'Gilead is mine and Man¦asseh · is ¦ mine:
Ephraim is my helmet and ¦ Judah · my ¦ rod · of‿com¦mand.

†9 'Moab is my wash-bowl over Edom will I ¦ cast my ¦ shoe:
against Philistia ¦ will I ¦ shout in ¦ triumph.'

10 Who will lead me into the ¦ forti·fied ¦ city:
who will ¦ bring me ¦ into ¦ Edom?

11 Have you not cast us ¦ off O ¦ God?:
you ¦ go not ¦ out · with our ¦ armies.

12 Give us your help a¦gainst the ¦ enemy:
for ¦ vain · is the ¦ help of ¦ man.

13 By the power of our God we ¦ shall do ¦ valiantly:
for it is he that ¦ will tread ¦ down our ¦ enemies.

109

1 O God of my praise do | not be | silent:
for evil and deceitful | mouths are | opened · a|gainst me.

2 They speak of me with | lying | tongues:
they surround me with words of hatred
they fight a|gainst me · with|out | cause.

3 In return for my friendship | they op|pose me:
and | that for · no | fault of | mine.

4 They repay me | evil · for | good:
and | hatred · for | my af|fection.

[5 Appoint an evil man to | stand a|gainst him:
and let an adversary | be at · his | right | hand.

6 When he is judged let him be | found | guilty:
let his prayer for | help be | counted · as | sin.

7 Let his | days be | few:
and let another | take what | he has | hoarded.

8 Let his children be | made | fatherless:
and his | wife be|come a | widow.

9 Let his children be | vagabonds · and | beggars:
let them seek alms | far · from their | own | homes.

10 Let the usurer exact | all · that he | has:
and let strangers | plunder · the | fruit · of his | toil.

11 Let no man be | loyal · to | him:
and let no one have | pity · on his | father·less | children.

12 Let his line be|come ex|tinct:
in one generation let their | name be | blotted | out.

13 Let the sins of his fathers be re|membered · by the | Lord:
and his mother's iniquity | not be | wiped a|way.

14 Let their sins be constantly be|fore the | Lord:
may he root out their | memo·ry | from the | earth.

15 For he was a man that did not remember to | show | loyalty:
but he persecuted the humble the poor and the‿crushed in spirit
and | sought to | put them · to | death.

16 He loved to curse * let curses | fall on | him:
he took no pleasure in blessing
so let | it be | far from | him.

17 He clothed himself in cursing | like a | garment:
so let it seep like water into his body
and like | oil | into · his | bones.

18 Let it be as the clothes he | wraps a|bout him:
or like the | girdle · that he | wears each | day.

[†] 19 This is the Lord's recompense to | those · that op|pose him:
to | those that · speak | evil · a|gainst me.]

20 Act for me O Lord my God for your | name's | sake:
and deliver me as your | steadfast | love is | good.

21 For I am | poor and | needy:
and my | heart | writhes with|in me.

22 I fade like a | lengthen·ing | shadow:
I am | shaken | off · like a | locust.

23 My knees are | weak from | fasting:
my | flesh grows | lean and | shrunken.

†24 I have become the | scorn of · my | enemies:
and when they see me they | toss their | heads ·
in de|rision.

25 Help me O | Lord my | God:
and save me | for your | mercy's | sake,

26 That men may know it was | your | hand:
that | you O | Lord have | done it.

27 Though they curse yet | give me · your | blessing:
and those that come against me will be put to shame
and your | servant | shall re|joice.

28 Let those that oppose me be | covered · with dis|grace:
let them | wear their | shame · as a | garment.

29 And I will give the Lord great | thanks · with my |
mouth:
and | praise him · in the | midst · of a | multitude.

30 For the Lord will stand at the right | hand · of the |
poor:
to save him from | those that | would con|demn him.

110

1 The Lord | said to | my lord:
'Sit at my right hand
until I | make your | enemies · your | footstool.'

2 The Lord commits to you the sceptre | of your | power
reign from | Zion · in the | midst of · your | enemies

3 Noble are you * from the day of your birth upon the holy | hill:
radiant are you even from the womb
in the | morning | dew of · your | youth.

4 The Lord has sworn and will | not turn | back:
'You are a priest for ever * after the | order | o
Mel|chizedek.'

5 The king shall stand at your right | hand O | Lord:
and shatter | kings · in the | day of · his | wrath.

6 Glorious in majesty * he shall judge a|mong the nations:
and shatter heads | over · a | wide | land.

†7 He shall slake his thirst from the brook be|side the way:
therefore shall | he lift | up his | head.

111

1 O praise the Lord
I will praise the Lord with my | whole | heart:
in the company of the upright
and a|mong the | congre|gation.

2 The works of the | Lord are | great:
and studied by | all who | take de|light in them.

3 His deeds are ma|jestic · and | glorious:
and his | righteous·ness | stands for | ever.

4 His marvellous acts have won him a name to | be re|membered:
the | Lord is | gracious · and | merciful.

5 He gives food to | those that | fear him:
he re|members · his | covenant · for | ever.

6 He showed his people the | power · of his | acts:
in giving them the | herit·age | of the | heathen.

7 The works of his hands are | faithful · and | just:
and | all · his com|mandments · are | sure;

8 They stand firm for | ever · and | ever:
they are done in | faithful·ness | and in | truth.

9 He sent redemption to his people
he ordained his | covenant · for | ever:
holy is his name and | worthy | to be | feared.

10 The fear of the Lord is the beginning of wisdom
and of good understanding are those that | keep · his com|mandments:
his | praise · shall en|dure for | ever.

112

1 O praise the Lord
Blessèd is the man who ˡ fears the ˡ Lord:
and greatly deˡlights in ˡ his comˡmandments.

2 His children shall be ˡ mighty · in the ˡ land:
a race of upright ˡ men who ˡ will be ˡ blessed.

3 Riches and plenty shall be ˡ in his ˡ house:
and his ˡ righteous·ness ˡ stands for ˡ ever.

4 Light arises in darkness ˡ for the ˡ upright:
gracious and merciful ˡ is the ˡ righteous ˡ man.

5 It goes well with the man who acts ˡ generously · and ˡ lends:
who ˡ guides · his afˡfairs with ˡ justice.

6 Surely he shall ˡ never · be ˡ moved:
the righteous shall be held in ˡ everˡlasting · reˡmembrance.

7 He will not ˡ fear bad ˡ tidings:
his heart is steadfast ˡ trusting ˡ in the ˡ Lord.

8 His heart is confident and ˡ will not ˡ fear:
he will see the ˡ downfall ˡ of his ˡ enemies.

9 He gives ˡ freely · to the ˡ poor:
his righteousness stands for ever
his ˡ head is · upˡlifted · in ˡ glory.

10 The wicked man shall see it ˡ and be ˡ angry:
he shall gnash his teeth and consume away
and the ˡ hope · of the ˡ wicked · shall ˡ fail.

113

1 Praise the Lord
O sing praises you that ˡ are his ˡ servants:
O ˡ praise the ˡ name · of the ˡ Lord.

2 Let the name of the ˡ Lord be ˡ blessed:
from this time ˡ forward ˡ and for ˡ ever.

3 From the rising of the sun to its ˡ going ˡ down:
let the ˡ name · of the ˡ Lord be ˡ praised.

4 The Lord is exalted over ˡ all the ˡ nations:
and his ˡ glory · is aˡbove the ˡ heavens.

5 Who can be likened to the ˡ Lord our ˡ God:
in ˡ heaven · or upˡon the ˡ earth,

6 Who has his ˡ dwelling · so ˡ high:
yet condescends to ˡ look on ˡ things beˡneath?

7 He raises the ˡ lowly · from theˡ dust:
and lifts the ˡ poor from ˡ out of · the ˡ dungheap;

8 He gives them a place aˡmong the ˡ princes:
even among the ˡ princes ˡ of his ˡ people.

†9 He causes the barren woman to ˡ keep ˡ house:
and makes her a joyful mother of children ˡ
Praise ˡ – the ˡ Lord.

114

1 When Israel came | out of | Egypt:
and the house of Jacob from among a | people · of an alien | tongue,

2 Judah be|came his | sanctuary:
and | Israel | his do|minion.

3 The sea saw | that and | fled:
Jor|dan was | driven | back.

4 The mountains | skipped like | rams:
and the little | hills like | young | sheep.

5 What ailed you O | sea · that you | fled:
O Jordan that | you were | driven | back?

6 You mountains that you | skipped like | rams:
and you little | hills like | young | sheep?

7 Tremble O earth at the | presence · of the | Lord:
at the | presence · of the | God of | Jacob,

8 Who turned the rock into a | pool of | water:
and the flint-stone | into · a | welling | spring.

115

1 Not to us O Lord not to us
but to your name ǀ give the ǀ glory:
for the sake of your faithfulness ǀ and your ǀ loving-ǀ kindness.

2 Why should the heathen say ǀ 'Where is · their ǀ God?':
our God is in heaven he ǀ does whatǀever · he ǀ wills.

3 As for their idols they are ǀ silver · and ǀ gold:
the ǀ work · of a ǀ man's ǀ hand.

4 They have ǀ mouths but ǀ speak not:
they have ǀ eyes · but they ǀ cannot ǀ see.

5 They have ears yet ǀ hear ǀ nothing:
they have ǀ noses · but ǀ cannot ǀ smell.

6 Hands they have but handle nothing
feet but they ǀ do not ǀ walk:
they ǀ make no ǀ sound · with their ǀ throats.

†7 Those who make them ǀ shall be ǀ like them:
so shall ǀ everyone · that ǀ trusts in ǀ them.

8 O Israel ǀ trust · in the ǀ Lord:
he is your ǀ help ǀ and your ǀ shield.

9 O house of Aaron ǀ trust · in the ǀ Lord:
he is your ǀ help ǀ and your ǀ shield.

10 You that fear the Lord ǀ trust · in the ǀ Lord:
he is your ǀ help ǀ and your ǀ shield.

11 The Lord has remembered us and ǀ he will ǀ bless us:
he will bless the house of Israel
he will ǀ bless the ǀ house of ǀ Aaron.

12 He will bless all those that ¦ fear the ¦ Lord:
both ¦ high and ¦ low to¦gether.

13 May the Lord in¦crease you ¦ greatly:
you ¦ and your ¦ children ¦ after you.

14 The blessing of the ¦ Lord · be up¦on you:
he that ¦ made ¦ heaven · and ¦ earth.

15 As for the heavens ¦ they · are the ¦ Lord's:
but the earth he has ¦ given · to the ¦ children · of ¦ men.

16 The dead do not ¦ praise the ¦ Lord:
nor do ¦ any · that go ¦ down to ¦ silence.

17 But we will ¦ bless the ¦ Lord:
both now and for evermore
O ¦ praise ¦ – the ¦ Lord.

116

1 I love the Lord because he ¦ heard my ¦ voice:
the ¦ voice of · my ¦ suppli¦cation;

2 Because he in¦clined his ¦ ear to me:
in the ¦ day ¦ that I ¦ called to him.

3 The cords of death encompassed me
the snares of the ¦ grave took ¦ hold on me:
I ¦ was in ¦ anguish · and ¦ sorrow.

4 Then I called upon the ¦ name · of the ¦ Lord:
'O ¦ Lord · I be¦seech you · de¦liver me!'

5 Gracious and righteous ǀ is the ǀ Lord:
full of comǀpassion ǀ is our ǀ God.

6 The Lord preǀserves the ǀ simple:
when ǀ I was · brought ǀ low he ǀ saved me.

7 Return O my ǀ soul · to your ǀ rest:
for the ǀ Lord ǀ has reǀwarded you.

8 For you O Lord have delivered my ǀ soul from ǀ death:
my eyes from ǀ tears · and my ǀ feet from ǀ falling.

†9 I will walk beǀfore the ǀ Lord:
in the ǀ land ǀ of the ǀ living.

10 I believed that I would perish I was ǀ brought · very ǀ low:
I said in my haste ǀ 'All ǀ men are ǀ liars.'

11 How shall I reǀpay the ǀ Lord:
for ǀ all his ǀ bene·fits ǀ to me?

12 I will take up the ǀ cup of · salǀvation:
and ǀ call up·on the ǀ name · of the ǀ Lord.

13 I will pay my ǀ vows · to the ǀ Lord:
in the ǀ presence · of ǀ all his ǀ people.

14 Grievous in the ǀ sight · of the ǀ Lord:
is the ǀ death ǀ of his ǀ faithful ones.

15 O Lord I am your servant
your servant and the ǀ son of · your ǀ handmaid:
you ǀ have unǀloosed my ǀ bonds.

16 I will offer you a sacrifice of ǀ thanksǀgiving:
and ǀ call up·on the ǀ name · of the ǀ Lord.

17 I will pay my ǀ vows · to the ǀ Lord:
in the ǀ presence · of ǀ all his ǀ people,

†18 In the courts of the ǀ house · of the ǀ Lord:
even in your midst O Jerusalem ǀ
Praise ǀ – the ǀ Lord.

117

1 O praise the Lord ǀ all you ǀ nations:
O ǀ praise him ǀ all you ǀ peoples.

2 For great is his loving-ǀkindness · toǀward us:
and the faithfulness of the Lord endures for ever ǀ
Praise ǀ – the ǀ Lord.

118

1 O give thanks to the Lord for ǀ he is ǀ good:
his ǀ mercy · enǀdures for ǀ ever.

2 Let Israel ǀ now proǀclaim:
that his ǀ mercy · enǀdures for ǀ ever.

3 Let the house of ǀ Aaron · proǀclaim:
that his ǀ mercy · enǀdures for ǀ ever.

4 Let those who fear the ǀ Lord proǀclaim:
that his ǀ mercy · enǀdures for ǀ ever.

5 In my danger I | called · to the | Lord:
he | answered · and | set me | free.

6 The Lord is on my side I | shall not | fear:
what can | man | do to | me?

7 The Lord is at my side | as my | helper:
I shall see the | downfall | of my | enemies.

8 It is better to take refuge | in the | Lord:
than to | put your | trust in | man;

†9 It is better to take refuge | in the | Lord:
than to | put your | trust in | princes.

10 All the | nations · sur|rounded me:
but in the name of the | Lord I | drove them | back.

11 They surrounded they surrounded me on | every | side:
but in the name of the | Lord I | drove them | back.

12 They swarmed about me like bees
they blazed like fire a|mong the | thorns:
in the name of the | Lord I | drove them | back.

13 I was pressed so hard that I | almost | fell:
but the | Lord | was my | helper.

†14 The Lord is my | strength · and my | song:
and has be|come | my sal|vation.

15 The sounds of | joy · and de|liverance:
are | in the | tents · of the | righteous.

16 The right hand of the Lord does | mighty | things:
the right hand of the | Lord | raises | up.

17 I shall not | die but | live:
and pro|claim the | works · of the | Lord.

18 The Lord has ˡ disciplined · me ˡ hard:
but he has not ˡ given · me ˡ over · to ˡ death.

19 Open me the ˡ gates of ˡ righteousness:
and I will enter and give ˡ thanks ˡ to the ˡ Lord.

20 This is the ˡ gate · of the ˡ Lord:
the ˡ righteous ˡ shall ˡ enter it.

21 I will praise you ˡ for you ˡ answered me:
and have beˡcome ˡ my salˡvation.

22 The stone that the ˡ builders · reˡjected:
has beˡcome the ˡ head · of the ˡ corner.

23 This is the ˡ Lord's ˡ doing:
and it is ˡ marvel·lous ˡ in our ˡ eyes.

24 This is the day that the ˡ Lord has ˡ made:
let us reˡjoice ˡ and be ˡ glad in it.

25 O Lord ˡ save us · we ˡ pray:
O Lord ˡ send ˡ us prosˡperity.

26 Blessèd is he who comes in the ˡ name · of the ˡ Lord
from the ˡ house · of the ˡ Lord we ˡ bless you.

27 The Lord is God and he has ˡ given · us ˡ light:
guide the festal throng up to the ˡ horns ˡ of the altar.

28 You are my God and ˡ I will ˡ praise you:
you are my ˡ God I ˡ will exˡalt you.

†29 O give thanks to the Lord for ˡ he is ˡ good:
and his ˡ mercy · enˡdures for ˡ ever.

119

1

1 Blessèd are those whose ˈ way is ˈ blameless:
who ˈ walk · in the ˈ law · of the ˈ Lord.

2 Blessèd are those who ˈ keep · his comˈmands:
and seek him ˈ with their ˈ whole ˈ heart;

3 Those who ˈ do no ˈ wrong:
but ˈ walk · in the ˈ ways of · our ˈ God.

4 For you Lord ˈ have comˈmanded us:
to perseˈvere in ˈ all your ˈ precepts.

5 If only my ˈ ways · were unˈerring:
towards the ˈ keeping ˈ of your ˈ statutes!

6 Then I should ˈ not · be aˈshamed:
when I ˈ looked on ˈ all · your comˈmandments.

7 I will praise you with sinˈcerity · of ˈ heart:
as I ˈ learn your ˈ righteous ˈ judgements.

8 I will ˈ keep your ˈ statutes:
O forˈsake me ˈ not ˈ utterly.

2

9 How shall a young man's ˈ path be ˈ pure:
unˈless he ˈ keep to · your ˈ word?

10 I have sought you with my ˈ whole ˈ heart:
let me not ˈ stray from ˈ your comˈmandments.

11 I have treasured your ˈ words · in my ˈ heart:
that I ˈ might not ˈ sin aˈgainst you.

12 Blessèd are ˈ you Lord ˈ God:
O ˈ teach me ˈ your ˈ statutes.

13 With my lips I ˈ have been ˈ telling:
all the ˈ judgements ˈ of your ˈ mouth;

14 And I find more joy in the way of ˈ your comˈmands:
than in ˈ all ˈ manner · of ˈ riches.

15 I will meditate ˈ on your ˈ precepts:
and give ˈ heed ˈ to your ˈ ways;

16 For my delight is wholly ˈ in your ˈ statutes:
and I will ˈ not forˈget your ˈ word.

3

17 O be bountiful to your servant that ˈ I may ˈ live:
in oˈbedi·ence ˈ to your ˈ word.

18 Take away the ˈ veil · from my ˈ eyes:
that I may see the ˈ wonders ˈ of your ˈ law.

19 I am but a ˈ stranger · on the ˈ earth:
do not ˈ hide · your comˈmandments ˈ from me.

20 My soul is conˈsumed with ˈ longing:
for your ˈ judgements ˈ day and ˈ night.

21 You have reˈbuked the ˈ proud:
and cursed are those who ˈ stray from ˈ your comˈmandments;

22 Turn away from me their reˈproach and ˈ scorn:
for ˈ I have ˈ kept · your comˈmands.

23 Though princes sit and plot toˈgether · aˈgainst me:
your servant shall ˈ medi·tate ˈ on your ˈ statutes:

24 For your commands are ˡ my deˡlight:
and they are ˡ counsellors · in ˡ my deˡfence.

4

25 I am humbled ˡ to the ˡ dust:
O give me life acˡcording ˡ to your ˡ word.

26 If I exˡamine · my ˡ ways:
surely you will answer me * O ˡ teach me ˡ your ˡ statutes!

27 Make me to understand the ˡ way of · your ˡ precepts:
and I shall meditate ˡ on your ˡ marvel·lous ˡ works.

28 My soul pines aˡway for ˡ sorrow:
O raise me up acˡcording ˡ to your ˡ word.

29 Keep me far from the ˡ way of · deˡception:
and ˡ grant me · the ˡ grace of · your ˡ law.

30 I have chosen the ˡ way of ˡ truth:
and have ˡ set your ˡ judgements · beˡfore me.

31 I hold fast to ˡ your comˡmands:
O Lord let me ˡ never ˡ be conˡfounded.

32 Let me run the way of ˡ your comˡmandments:
for ˡ you will ˡ liberate · my ˡ heart.

5

33 Teach me O Lord the ˡ way of · your ˡ statutes:
and I will ˡ honour · it ˡ to the ˡ end.

34 Give me understanding that I may ˡ keep your ˡ law:
that I may keep it ˡ with my ˡ whole ˡ heart.

35 Guide me in the path of ˡ your comˡmandments:
for thereˡin is ˡ my deˡlight.

36 Incline my heart to ꞁ your comꞁmands:
and ꞁ not to ꞁ selfish ꞁ gain.

37 Turn away my eyes from ꞁ looking · on ꞁ vanities:
as I walk in your ꞁ way ꞁ give me ꞁ life.

38 Make good your promise ꞁ to your ꞁ servant:
the promise that enꞁdures for ꞁ all who ꞁ fear you.

39 Turn aside the ꞁ taunts · that I ꞁ dread:
for your ꞁ judgements · are ꞁ very ꞁ good.

40 Lord I ꞁ long for · your ꞁ precepts:
in your ꞁ righteous·ness ꞁ give me ꞁ life.

6

41 Let your loving mercy come to ꞁ me O ꞁ Lord:
and your salvation acꞁcording ꞁ to your ꞁ word.

42 Then I shall have an answer for ꞁ those · who reꞁproach me:
for I ꞁ trust ꞁ in your ꞁ word.

43 Do not take the word of truth utterly ꞁ out of · my mouth:
for in your ꞁ judgements ꞁ is my ꞁ hope.

44 Let me keep your ꞁ law conꞁtinually:
O ꞁ let me ꞁ keep it · for ꞁ ever.

45 And so I shall ꞁ walk at ꞁ liberty:
beꞁcause · I have ꞁ sought your ꞁ precepts.

46 I shall speak of your comꞁmands be·fore ꞁ kings:
and shall ꞁ not be ꞁ put to ꞁ shame.

47 My delight shall be in ꞁ your comꞁmandments:
which ꞁ I have ꞁ greatly ꞁ loved;

48 I shall worship you with ¦ outstretched ¦ hands:
and I shall ¦ medi·tate ¦ on your ¦ statutes.

7

49 Remember your ¦ word · to your ¦ servant:
on ¦ which · you have ¦ built my ¦ hope.

50 This has been my comfort in ¦ my af¦fliction:
for your ¦ word has ¦ brought me ¦ life.

51 Though the proud have ¦ laughed me · to ¦ scorn:
I have not ¦ turned a¦side from · your ¦ law;

52 But I called to mind O Lord your ¦ judgements · of ¦ old:
and in ¦ them · I have ¦ found · consol¦ation.

53 I am seized with indignation ¦ at the ¦ wicked:
for ¦ they have · for¦saken · your ¦ law.

54 But your statutes have be¦come my ¦ songs:
in the ¦ house ¦ of my ¦ pilgrimage.

55 I think on your name O ¦ Lord · in the ¦ night:
and ¦ I ob¦serve your ¦ law;

56 This has ¦ been · my re¦ward:
be¦cause · I have ¦ kept your ¦ precepts.

8

57 The Lord ¦ is my ¦ portion:
I have ¦ promised · to ¦ keep your ¦ words.

58 I have sought your favour with my ¦ whole ¦ heart:
O be gracious to me ac¦cording ¦ to your ¦ word.

59 I have taken ¦ stock of · my ¦ ways:
and have turned back my ¦ feet to ¦ your com¦mands.

60 I made haste and did ˈ not deˈlay:
to ˈ keep ˈ your comˈmandments.

61 The snares of the ˈ wicked · enˈcompassed me:
but I did ˈ not forˈget your ˈ law;

62 At midnight I rise to ˈ give you ˈ thanks:
for the ˈ righteous·ness ˈ of your ˈ judgements.

63 I am a friend to ˈ all who ˈ fear you:
to ˈ those who ˈ keep your ˈ precepts.

64 The earth O Lord is full of your ˈ loving ˈ mercy:
O ˈ teach me ˈ your ˈ statutes.

9

65 Lord you have done ˈ good to · your ˈ servant:
in acˈcordance ˈ with your ˈ word.

66 O teach me right ˈ judgement · and ˈ knowledge:
for I ˈ trust in ˈ your comˈmandments.

67 Before I was afflicted I ˈ went aˈstray:
but ˈ now I ˈ keep your ˈ word.

68 You are good and you ˈ do ˈ good:
O ˈ teach me ˈ your ˈ statutes.

69 The proud have ˈ smeared me · with ˈ lies:
but I will keep your precepts ˈ with my ˈ whole ˈ
heart.

70 Their hearts are ˈ gross like ˈ fat:
but my deˈlight is ˈ in your ˈ law.

71 It is good for me that ˈ I was · afˈflicted:
so ˈ I might ˈ learn your ˈ statutes.

72 The law of your mouth is | dearer · to | me:
than a | wealth of | gold and | silver.

10

73 Your hands have | made me · and | fashioned me:
O give me understanding‿
that | I may | learn · your com|mandments.

74 Those who fear you shall see me | and re|joice:
for my | hope is | in your | word.

75 I know Lord that your | judgements · are | right:
and that in | faithfulness · you | have af|flicted me.

76 Let your merciful kindness | be my | comfort:
according to your | promise | to your | servant.

77 O let your mercy come to me that | I may | live:
for your | law is | my de|light.

78 Let the proud be shamed
who steal my | rights · through their | lies:
but I will | |medi·tate | on your | precepts.

79 Let those who fear you | turn to | me:
and | they shall | know · your com|mands.

80 O let my heart be | sound in · your | statutes:
that I may | never · be | put to | shame.

11

81 My soul languishes for | your sal|vation:
but my | hope is | in your | word;

82 My eyes fail with | watching · for your | promise:
saying 'O | when | will you | comfort me?'

83 I am parchèd as a wineskin | in the | smoke:
yet I do | not for|get your | statutes.

84 How many are the | days of · your | servant:
and | when · will you | judge my | persecutors?

85 The proud have dug | pitfalls | for me:
in de|fiance | of your | law.

86 All your com|mandments · are | true:
but they persecute me with lies * O | come | to my
help!

87 They have almost made an end of me | on the | earth:
but I have | not for|saken · your | precepts.

88 In your merciful goodness | give me | life:
that I may keep the com|mands | of your | mouth.

12

89 Lord your | word · is for | ever:
it stands | firm | in the | heavens.

90 Your faithfulness abides from one gener|ation · to
an|other:
firm as the | earth which | you have | made.

91 As for your judgements they stand | fast this | day:
for | all things | are your | servants.

92 If your law had not been | my de|light:
I would have | perished · in | my af|fliction.

93 I will never for|get your | precepts:
for by | them · you have | given · me | life.

94 I am | yours O | save me:
for | I have | sought your | precepts.

95 The wicked have lain in wait for me | to de|stroy me:
but I | think on | your com|mands.

96 I have seen that all perfection | comes · to an | end:
only your com|mandment | has no | bounds.

13

97 Lord how I | love your | law:
it is my medi|tation | all the · day | long.

98 Your commandments have made me wiser | than my | enemies:
for they re|main with | me for | ever.

99 I have more understanding than | all my | teachers:
for I | study | your com|mands.

100 I am wiser | than the | agèd:
be|cause · I have | kept your | precepts.

101 I have held back my feet from every | evil | path:
that | I might | keep your | word;

102 I have not turned a|side from · your | judgements:
for | you your|self are · my | teacher.

103 How sweet are your | words · to my | tongue:
sweeter than | honey | to my | mouth.

104 Through your precepts I get | under|standing:
therefore I | hate all | lying | ways.

14

105 Your word is a lantern ˈ to my ˈ feet:
and a ˈ light ˈ to my ˈ path.

106 I have vowed and ˈ sworn an ˈ oath:
to ˈ keep your ˈ righteous ˈ judgements.

107 I have been afflicted beˈyond ˈ measure:
Lord give me life acˈcording ˈ to your ˈ word.

108 Accept O Lord the freewill offerings ˈ of my ˈ mouth:
and ˈ teach me ˈ your ˈ judgements.

109 I take my life in my ˈ hands conˈtinually:
yet I do ˈ not forˈget your ˈ law.

110 The wicked have ˈ laid a ˈ snare for me:
but I ˈ have not ˈ strayed from · your ˈ precepts.

111 Your commands are my inˈheritance · for ˈ ever:
they ˈ are the ˈ joy of · my ˈ heart.

112 I have set my heart to fulˈfil your ˈ statutes:
always ˈ even ˈ to the ˈ end.

15

113 I loathe those who are ˈ double-ˈminded:
but your ˈ law ˈ do I ˈ love.

114 You are my shelter ˈ and my ˈ shield:
and in your ˈ word ˈ is my ˈ hope.

115 Away from me all ˈ you that · do ˈ evil:
I will keep the comˈmandments ˈ of my ˈ God.

116 Be my stay according to your word that ˈ I may ˈ live:
and do not disapˈpoint me ˈ in my ˈ hope.

117 Hold me up and I ǀ shall be ǀ safe:
and I will ever deǀlight ǀ in your ǀ statutes.

118 You scorn all those who ǀ swerve from · your ǀ statutes:
for their ǀ calumnies · aǀgainst me · are ǀ lies;

119 All the ungodly of the earth you ǀ count as ǀ dross:
therefore I ǀ love ǀ your comǀmands.

120 My flesh ǀ shrinks for ǀ fear of you:
and I am aǀfraid ǀ of your ǀ judgements.

16

121 I have done what is ǀ just and ǀ right:
O do not give me ǀ over · to ǀ my opǀpressors.

122 Stand surety for your ǀ servant's ǀ good:
let ǀ not the ǀ proud opǀpress me.

123 My eyes fail with watching for ǀ your salǀvation:
for the fulfilment ǀ of your ǀ righteous ǀ word.

124 O deal with your servant according to your ǀ loving mercy:
and ǀ teach me ǀ your ǀ statutes.

125 I am your servant O give me ǀ underǀstanding:
that ǀ I may ǀ know · your comǀmands.

126 It is time for the ǀ Lord to ǀ act:
for they ǀ viol·ate ǀ your ǀ law.

127 Therefore I ǀ love · your comǀmandments:
more than gold ǀ more · than the ǀ finest ǀ gold;

128 Therefore I straighten my paths by ǀ all your ǀ precepts:
and I ǀ hate all ǀ lying ǀ ways.

17

129 Wonderful are | your com|mands:
and | therefore · my | soul | keeps them.

130 The unfolding of your | word gives | light:
it gives under|standing | to the | simple.

131 I open my mouth and draw | in my | breath:
for I | yearn for | your com|mandments.

132 O turn to me and be | merci·ful | to me:
as is your way with | those who | love your | name.

133 Order my steps according | to your | word:
that no evil | may get | master·y | over me.

134 Deliver me from | man's op|pression:
that | I may | keep your | precepts.

135 Make your face shine up|on your | servant:
and | teach me | your | statutes.

136 My eyes gush out with | streams of | water:
because they | pay no | heed to · your | law.

18

137 Righteous are | you Lord | God:
and | just are | your | judgements;

138 The commands that | you · have com|manded:
are ex|ceeding·ly | righteous · and | true.

139 Zeal and indignation have | choked my | mouth:
because my enemies | have for|gotten · your | words.

140 Your word has been | tried · in the | fire:
and | therefore · your | servant | loves it.

141 I am small and of ¦ no ac¦count:
but I have ¦ not for¦gotten · your ¦ precepts.

142 Your righteousness is an ever¦lasting ¦ righteousness:
and your ¦ law ¦ is the ¦ truth.

143 Trouble and anguish have ¦ taken ¦ hold on me:
but your com¦mandments · are ¦ my de¦light.

144 The righteousness of your commands is ¦ ever¦lasting:
O give me under¦standing · and ¦ I shall ¦ live.

19

145 I call with my ¦ whole ¦ heart:
hear me O Lord ¦ I will ¦ keep your ¦ statutes.

146 I cry out to ¦ you O ¦ save me:
and ¦ I will ¦ heed · your com¦mands.

147 Before the morning light I ¦ rise · and I ¦ call:
for in your ¦ word ¦ is my ¦ hope.

148 Before the night watch my ¦ eyes ¦ wake:
that I may ¦ meditate · up¦on your ¦ words.

149 Hear my voice O Lord in your ¦ loving ¦ mercy:
and according to your ¦ judgements ¦ give me ¦ life.

150 They draw near to me who mal¦icious·ly ¦ persecute me:
but ¦ they are ¦ far from · your ¦ law.

151 You Lord are ¦ close at ¦ hand:
and ¦ all · your com¦mandments · are ¦ true.

152 I have known long since from ¦ your com¦mands:
that you have ¦ founded ¦ them for ¦ ever.

20

153 Consider my affliction | and de|liver me:
for I do | not for|get your | law.

154 Plead my cause and | set me | free:
O give me life ac|cording | to your | word.

155 Salvation is | far · from the | wicked:
for they | do not | seek your | statutes.

156 Numberless O Lord are your | tender | mercies:
according to your | judgements | give me | life.

157 Many there are that persecute | me and | trouble me:
but I have not | swerved from | your com|mands.

158 I am cut to the heart when I | see the | faithless:
for they | do not | keep your | word.

159 Consider O Lord how I | love your | precepts:
and in your | mercy | give me | life.

160 The sum of your | word is | truth:
and all your righteous | judgements | stand for | ever.

21

161 Princes have persecuted me with|out a | cause:
but my heart | stands in | awe of · your | word.

162 I am as | glad of · your | word:
as | one who | finds rich | spoil.

163 Lies I | hate · and ab|hor:
but your | law | do I | love.

164 Seven times a | day I | praise you:
be|cause of · your | righteous | judgements.

165 Great is the peace of those who | love your | law:
and | nothing · shall | make them | stumble.

166 Lord I have waited for | your sal|vation:
and I have | done | your com|mandments.

167 My soul has heeded | your com|mands:
and I | love them · be|yond | measure.

168 I have kept your precepts | and com|mands:
for all my | ways are | open · be|fore you.

22

169 Let my cry | come to you · O | Lord:
O give me understanding ac|cording | to your | word;

170 Let my supplication | come be|fore you:
and deliver me ac|cording | to your | promise.

171 My lips shall pour | forth your | praise:
be|cause you | teach me · your | statutes;

172 My tongue shall | sing of · your | word:
for | all · your com|mandments · are | righteousness.

173 Let your hand be | swift to | help me:
for | I have | chosen · your | precepts.

174 Lord I have longed for | your sal|vation:
and your | law is | my de|light.

175 O let my soul live that | I may | praise you:
and let your | judgements | be my | help.

176 I have gone astray like a | sheep · that is | lost:
O seek your servant
for I do | not for|get · your com|mandments.

120

1 I call to the ǀ Lord · in my ǀ trouble:
that ǀ he may ǀ answer ǀ me.

2 O Lord deliver me from ǀ lying ǀ lips:
and ǀ from the ǀ treacher·ous ǀ tongue.

3 What will he do to you
and what more will he do to you O ǀ treacher·ous tongue?:
you are sharp as the arrows of a warrior
that are ǀ tempered · in ǀ coals of ǀ juniper.

4 Alas for me * I am like a ǀ stranger · in ǀ Meshech:
like one who dwells aǀmidst the ǀ tents of ǀ Kedar.

5 My soul has ǀ been too ǀ long:
among ǀ those · who are ǀ enemies · to ǀ peace.

6 I am for peace but ǀ when I ǀ speak of it:
they ǀ make them·selves ǀ ready · for ǀ war.

121

1 I lift up my ǀ eyes · to the ǀ hills:
but ǀ where · shall I ǀ find ǀ help?

2 My help ǀ comes · from the ǀ Lord:
who has ǀ made ǀ heaven · and ǀ earth.

3 He will not suffer your ǀ foot to ǀ stumble:
and he who watches ǀ over · you ǀ will not ǀ sleep.

4 Be sure he who has | charge of | Israel:
will | neither | slumber · nor | sleep.

5 The Lord him|self is · your | keeper:
the Lord is your defence up|on your | right | hand;

6 The sun shall not | strike you · by | day:
nor | shall the | moon by | night.

7 The Lord will defend you from | all | evil:
it is | he · who will | guard your | life.

8 The Lord will defend your going out and your |
coming | in:
from this time | forward · for | ever|more.

122

1 I was glad when they | said to | me:
'Let us | go · to the | house · of the | Lord.'

2 And now our | feet are | standing:
with|in your | gates · O Je|rusalem;

†3 Jerusalem which is | built · as a | city:
where the | pilgrims | gather · in | unity.

4 There the tribes go up the | tribes · of the | Lord:
as he commanded Israel
to give | thanks · to the | name · of the | Lord.

5 There are set | thrones of | judgement:
the | thrones · of the | house of | David.

6 O pray for the | peace · of Je|rusalem:
may | those who | love you | prosper.

7 Peace be with|in your | walls:
and pros|peri·ty | in your | palaces.

8 For the sake of my brothers | and com|panions:
I will | pray that | peace be | with you.

9 For the sake of the house of the | Lord our | God:
I will | seek | for your | good.

123

1 To you I lift | up my | eyes:
you who are en|throned | in the | heavens.

2 As the eyes of servants look to the | hand of · their | master:
or as the eyes of a maid to|ward the | hand of · her | mistress,

†3 So our eyes look to the | Lord our | God:
un|til he | show us · his | mercy.

4 Have mercy upon us O Lord have | mercy · up|on us:
for we have | had our | fill · of de|rision.

5 Our souls overflow with the mockery of | those at | ease:
and with the | contempt | of the | proud.

124

1 If the Lord had not been on our side
now may | Israel | say:
if the Lord had not been on our side‿
when | men rose | up a|gainst us,

2 Then they would have | swallowed us · a|live:
when their | anger · was | kindled · a|gainst us.

3 Then the waters would have overwhelmed us
and the | torrent · gone | over us:
the raging waters | would have | gone clean | over us.

4 But praised | be the | Lord:
who has not given us as a | prey | to their | teeth.

5 We have escaped like a bird from the | snare · of the | fowler:
the snare is | broken · and | we have · gone | free.

6 Our help is in the | name · of the | Lord:
who has | made | heaven · and | earth.

125

1 Those who put their trust in the Lord‿
shall | be as · Mount | Zion:
which cannot be | shaken · but en|dures for | ever.

2 As the mountains stand about Jerusalem
so stands the Lord a|bout his | people:
from this time | forward · for | ever|more.

3 For the sceptre of wickedness shall have no sway
over the land apportioned | to the | righteous:
lest the righteous | set their | hands to · do | evil.

4 Do good O Lord to | those · who are | good:
to | those · that are | upright · in | heart.

†5 As for those who turn aside to crooked ways
let the Lord lead them away with the | evil|doers
and in | Israel | let there · be | peace.

126

1 When the Lord turned again the | fortunes · of | Zion
then were we like | men re|stored to | life.

2 Then was our mouth | filled with | laughter:
and | our | tongue with | singing.

3 Then said they a|mong the | heathen:
'The Lord has | done great | things for | them.'

4 Truly the Lord has done great | things for | us:
and | therefore | we re|joiced.

5 Turn again our | fortunes · O | Lord:
as the streams re|turn · to the | dry | south.

6 Those that | sow in | tears:
shall | reap with | songs of | joy.

†7 He who goes out weeping | bearing · the | seed:
shall come again in gladness | ‿
bringing · his | sheaves | with him.

127

1 Unless the Lord ˡ builds the ˡ house:
their labour ˡ is but ˡ lost that ˡ build it.

2 Unless the Lord ˡ keeps the ˡ city:
the ˡ watchmen ˡ watch in ˡ vain.

3 It is in vain that you rise up early and go so late to rest
eating the ˡ bread of ˡ toil:
for the Lord bestows honour ˡ and on ˡ those ·‿
whom he ˡ loves.

4 Behold children are a heritage ˡ from the ˡ Lord:
and the ˡ fruit · of the ˡ womb is · his ˡ gift.

5 Like arrows in the ˡ hand · of a ˡ warrior:
are the ˡ sons · of a ˡ man's ˡ youth.

6 Happy the man who has his ˡ quiver ˡ full of them:
he will not be put to shame
when he confronts his ˡ enem·ies ˡ at the ˡ gate.

128

1 Blessèd is everyone who ˡ fears the ˡ Lord:
and walks in the ˡ confine ˡ of his ˡ ways.

2 You will eat the ˡ fruit of · your ˡ labours:
happy shall you ˡ be and ˡ all · shall go ˡ well with you.

3 Your wife withˡin your ˡ house:
shall ˡ be · as a ˡ fruitful ˡ vine;

4 Your children a¦round your ¦ table:
like the fresh ¦ shoots ¦ of the ¦ olive.

5 Behold thus shall the ¦ man be ¦ blessed:
who ¦ lives · in the ¦ fear · of the ¦ Lord.

6 May the Lord so ¦ bless you · from ¦ Zion:
that you see Jerusalem in prosperity ¦‿
all the ¦ days of · your ¦ life.

†7 May you see your ¦ children's ¦ children:
and in ¦ Israel ¦ let there · be ¦ peace.

129

1 Many a time from my youth upward have they ¦ fought
against me:
now ¦ may ¦ Israel ¦ say,

2 Many a time from my youth upward have they ¦fought
a¦gainst me:
but ¦ they have ¦ not pre¦vailed.

3 They have scored my back as ¦ with a ¦ ploughshare:
they have ¦ opened ¦ long ¦ furrows.

4 But the ¦ Lord is ¦ righteous:
and he has cut me ¦ free · from the ¦ thongs · of the
wicked.

5 They shall be confounded and ¦ turned ¦ backward:
all ¦ those who ¦ hate ¦ Zion.

6 They shall be as the grass that grows up¦on the
housetops:
which withers before it ¦ comes to ¦ any ¦ good,

7 With which no reaper may ˡ fill his ˡ hand:
nor the ˡ binder · of ˡ sheaves his ˡ bosom.

8 And none who pass by shall say to them
'The blessing of the ˡ Lord · be upˡon you:
we ˡ bless you · in the ˡ name · of the ˡ Lord.'

130

1 Out of the depths have I called to ˡ you O ˡ Lord:
Lord ˡ hear ˡ my ˡ voice;

2 O let your ears conˡsider ˡ well:
the ˡ voice · of my ˡ suppliˡcation.

3 If you Lord should note what ˡ we do ˡ wrong:
who ˡ then O ˡ Lord could ˡ stand?

4 But there is forˡgiveness · with ˡ you:
so that ˡ you ˡ shall be ˡ feared.

5 I wait for the Lord * my ˡ soul ˡ waits for him:
and ˡ in his ˡ word · is my ˡ hope.

6 My soul ˡ looks · for the ˡ Lord:
more than watchmen for the morning
more I say than ˡ watchmen ˡ for the ˡ morning.

7 O Israel trust in the Lord * for with the ˡ Lord ·‿
there is ˡ mercy:
and with ˡ him is ˡ ample · reˡdemption.

8 He will reˡdeem ˡ Israel:
from the ˡ multi·tude ˡ of his ˡ sins.

131

1 O Lord my | heart is · not | proud:
nor | are my | eyes | haughty.

2 I do not busy myself in | great | matters:
or in | things too | wonder·ful | for me.

3 But I have calmed and quieted my soul
like a weaned child upon its | mother's | breast:
like a child on its mother's breast |‿
is my | soul with|in me.

4 O Israel | trust · in the | Lord:
from this time | forward | and for | ever.

132

1 Lord remember David and | all his | trouble:
how he swore an oath to the Lord
and vowed to the | Mighty | One of | Jacob;

2 'I will not enter the | shelter · of my | house:
nor climb into the | comfort | of my | bed;

3 'I will not give | sleep to · my | eyes:
or | slumber | to my | eyelids,

4 'Till I find out a place for the | ark · of the | Lord:
a dwelling for the | Mighty | One of | Jacob.'

5 Lo we | heard of it · at | Ephrathah:
we | found it · in the | fields of | Ja-ar.

6 Let us go to the | place of · his | dwelling:
let us fall upon our | knees be|fore his | footstool.

7 Arise O Lord | into · your | resting-place:
you | and the | ark of · your | might.

8 Let your priests be | clothed with | righteousness:
and let your | faithful · ones | shout for | joy.

†9 For the sake of | David · your | servant:
do not turn away the | face of | your an|ointed.

10 The Lord has | sworn to | David:
an | oath · which he | will not | break;

11 'One who is the | fruit of · your | body:
I will | set up|on your | throne.

12 'If your children will keep my covenant
and the com|mands · which I | teach them:
their children also shall sit up|on your | throne for | ever.'

13 For the Lord has chosen | Zion · for him|self:
he has de|sired it · for his | habi|tation.

14 'This shall be my | resting-place · for | ever:
here will I dwell for | my de|light · is in | her.

15 'I will bless her pro|visions · with a|bundance:
I will | satisfy · her | poor with | bread.

16 'I will clothe her | priests with · sal|vation:
and her | faithful ones · shall | shout for | joy.

17 'There will I make a horn to sprout‿
for the | family · of | David:
I have prepared a | lamp for | my an|ointed.

†18 'As for his enemies I will | cover them · with | shame:
but upon his | head · shall his | crown be | bright.'

133

1 Behold how good and how ˡ lovely · it ˡ is:
when brothers ˡ live toˡgether · in ˡ unity.

2 It is fragrant as oil upon the head
that runs down ˡ over · the ˡ beard:
fragrant as oil upon the beard of Aaron
that ran down over the ˡ collar ˡ of his ˡ robe.

3 It is like a ˡ dew of ˡ Hermon:
like the dew that falls upˡon the ˡ hill of ˡ Zion.

4 For there the Lord has comˡmanded · his ˡ blessing:
which is ˡ life for ˡ everˡmore.

134

1 Come bless the Lord all you ˡ servants · of the ˡ Lord:
you that by night ˡ stand · in the ˡ house of · our ˡ God.

2 Lift up your hands toward the holy place‿
and ˡ bless the ˡ Lord:
may the Lord bless you from Zion
the ˡ Lord who · made ˡ heaven · and ˡ earth.

135

1 Praise the Lord
praise the ˈ name · of the ˈ Lord:
praise him you ˈ servants ˈ of the ˈ Lord,

2 Who stand in the ˈ house · of the ˈ Lord:
in the ˈ courts · of the ˈ house of · our ˈ God.

3 Praise the Lord for the ˈ Lord is ˈ gracious:
sing praises to his ˈ name for ˈ it is ˈ good.

4 For the Lord has chosen Jacob ˈ for himˈself:
and Israel ˈ as his ˈ own posˈsession.

5 I know that the ˈ Lord is ˈ great:
and that our ˈ Lord · is aˈbove all ˈ gods.

6 He does whatever he wills * in heaven and upˈon the ˈ earth:
in the seas and ˈ in the ˈ great ˈ depths.

7 He brings up clouds from the ˈ ends · of the ˈ earth:
he makes lightning for the rain
and brings the ˈ wind ˈ out of · his ˈ storehouses.

8 He struck down the ˈ firstborn · of ˈ Egypt:
both ˈ man and ˈ beast aˈlike.

9 He sent signs and wonders into your ˈ midst O ˈ Egypt:
against Pharaoh and aˈgainst ˈ all his ˈ servants.

10 He struck down ˈ great ˈ nations:
and ˈ slew ˈ mighty ˈ kings,

11 Sihon king of the Amorites and Og the ˈ king of ˈ Bashan:
and ˈ all the ˈ princes · of ˈ Canaan.

12 He made over their ˈ land · as a ˈ heritage:
a ˈ heritage · for ˈ Israel · his ˈ people.

13 O Lord your name shall enˈdure for ˈ ever:
so shall your renown throughˈout all ˈ generˈations.

14 For the Lord will ˈ vindicate · his ˈ people:
he will take ˈ pity ˈ on his ˈ servants.

15 As for the idols of the nations
they are but ˈ silver · and ˈ gold:
the ˈ work · of a ˈ man's ˈ hand.

16 They have ˈ mouths but ˈ speak not:
they have ˈ eyes · but they ˈ cannot ˈ see.

17 They have ears yet ˈ hear ˈ nothing:
there is no ˈ breath ˈ in their ˈ nostrils.

18 Those who make them ˈ shall be ˈ like them:
so shall ˈ everyˈone that ˈ trusts in them.

19 Bless the Lord O ˈ house of ˈ Israel:
bless the ˈ Lord O ˈ house of ˈ Aaron.

20 Bless the Lord O ˈ house of ˈ Levi:
you that ˈ fear the · Lord ˈ bless the ˈ Lord.

†21 Blessèd be the ˈ Lord from ˈ Zion:
he that dwells in Jerusalem ˈ
Praise ˈ – the ˈ Lord.

136

1 O give thanks to the Lord for ˈ he is ˈ good:
for his ˈ mercy · enˈdures for ˈ ever.

2 O give thanks to the ˈ God of ˈ gods:
for his ˈ mercy · enˈdures for ˈ ever.

†3 O give thanks to the ˈ Lord of ˈ lords:
for his ˈ mercy · enˈdures for ˈ ever;

4 To him who alone does ˈ great ˈ wonders:
for his ˈ mercy · enˈdures for ˈ ever;

5 Who by wisdom ˈ made the ˈ heavens:
for his ˈ mercy · enˈdures for ˈ ever;

6 Who stretched out the earth upˈon the ˈ waters:
for his ˈ mercy · enˈdures for ˈ ever;

7 Who made the ˈ great ˈ lights:
for his ˈ mercy · enˈdures for ˈ ever,

8 The sun to ˈ rule the ˈ day:
for his ˈ mercy · enˈdures for ˈ ever,

9 The moon and the stars to ˈ govern · the ˈ night:
for his ˈ mercy · enˈdures for ˈ ever;

10 Who struck down Egypt ˈ and its ˈ firstborn:
for his ˈ mercy · enˈdures for ˈ ever;

11 Who brought out Israel ˈ from aˈmong them:
for his ˈ mercy · enˈdures for ˈ ever,

†12 With a strong hand and with ˈ outstretched ˈ arm:
for his ˈ mercy · enˈdures for ˈ ever;

13 Who divided the Red Sea into | two | parts:
for his | mercy · en|dures for | ever,

14 And made Israel pass | through the | midst of it:
for his | mercy · en|dures for | ever;

15 Who cast off Pharaoh and his host into the | Red | Sea:
for his | mercy · en|dures for | ever;

16 Who led his people | through the | wilderness:
for his | mercy · en|dures for | ever;

17 Who struck down | great | kings:
for his | mercy · en|dures for | ever;

18 Who slew | mighty | kings:
for his | mercy · en|dures for | ever,

19 Sihon | king · of the | Amorites:
for his | mercy · en|dures for | ever,

20 And Og the | king of | Bashan:
for his | mercy · en|dures for | ever;

21 Who made over their | land · as a heritage:
for his | mercy · en|dures for | ever,

22 As a heritage for | Israel · his | servant:
for his | mercy · en|dures for | ever;

23 Who remembered us in our hu|mili|ation:
for his | mercy · en|dures for | ever,

24 And delivered us | from our | enemies:
for his | mercy · en|dures for | ever;

25 Who gives food to | all that | lives:
for his | mercy · en|dures for | ever.

26 O give thanks to the ǀ God of ǀ heaven:
for his ǀ mercy · en ǀ dures for ǀ ever.

137

1 By the waters of Babylon we sat ǀ down and ǀ wept:
when ǀ we re ǀ membered ǀ Zion.

2 As for our harps we ǀ hung them ǀ up:
upon the ǀ trees · that are ǀ in that ǀ land.

3 For there those who led us away captive‿
re ǀ quired of us · a ǀ song:
and those who had despoiled us demanded mirth
saying 'Sing us ǀ one of · the ǀ songs of ǀ Zion.'

*4 How can we sing the Lord's ǀ song · in a ǀ strange ǀ land?

5 If I forget you ǀ O Je ǀ rusalem:
let my right ǀ hand for ǀ get its ǀ mastery.

6 Let my tongue cling to the ǀ roof of · my ǀ mouth:
if I do not remember you
if I do not prefer Jerusalem a ǀ bove my ǀ chief ǀ joy.

[7 Remember O Lord against the Edomites‿
the ǀ day · of Je ǀ rusalem:
how they said 'Down with it down with it ǀ
raze it · to ǀ its found ǀ ations.'

* sung to the last four bars of the chant.

8 O daughter of Babylon ꞁ you that · lay ꞁ waste:
happy shall he be who serves ꞁ you as ꞁ you hav
served ꞁ us;

[†]9 Happy shall he be who ꞁ takes your ꞁ little ones:
and ꞁ dashes them · aꞁgainst the ꞁ stones.]

138

1 I will give you thanks O Lord with my ꞁ whole ꞁ hea
even before the ꞁ gods · will I ꞁ sing your ꞁ praise

2 I will bow down toward your holy temple
and give ꞁ thanks to · your ꞁ name:
because of your faithfulness and your loving-kindn
for you have made your name and your ꞁ wo
suꞁpreme · over ꞁ all things.

3 At a time when I called to you you ꞁ gave me ꞁ answe
and put new ꞁ strength withꞁin my ꞁ soul.

4 All the kings of the earth shall ꞁ praise you · O ꞁ Lor
for they have ꞁ heard the ꞁ words of · your ꞁ mouth

5 And they shall sing of the ꞁ ways · of the ꞁ Lord:
that the ꞁ glory · of the ꞁ Lord is ꞁ great.

6 For though the Lord is exalted he looks upꞁon the
lowly:
but he ꞁ humbles · the ꞁ proud · from aꞁfar.

7 Though I walk in the midst of danger
yet will you pre¦serve my ¦ life:
you will stretch out your hand‿
against the fury of my enemies
and ¦ your right ¦ hand shall ¦ save me.

8 The Lord will complete his ¦ purpose ¦ for me:
your loving-kindness O Lord endures for ever
do not forsake the ¦ work · of your ¦ own ¦ hands.

139

1 O Lord you have searched me ¦ out and ¦ known me:
you know when I sit or when I stand
you comprehend my ¦ thoughts ¦ long be¦fore.

2 You discern my path and the places ¦ where I ¦ rest:
you are ac¦quainted · with ¦ all my ¦ ways.

3 For there is not a ¦ word · on my ¦ tongue:
but you Lord ¦ know it ¦ alto¦gether.

4 You have encompassed me be¦hind · and be¦fore:
and have ¦ laid your ¦ hand up¦on me.

†5 Such knowledge is too ¦ wonder·ful ¦ for me:
so ¦ high · that I ¦ cannot · en¦dure it.

6 Where shall I ¦ go · from your ¦ spirit:
or where shall I ¦ flee ¦ from your ¦ presence?

7 If I ascend into heaven ¦ you are ¦ there:
if I make my bed in the grave ¦ you are ¦ there ¦ also.

8 If I spread out my wings to¦wards the ¦ morning:
or dwell in the ¦ utter·most ¦ parts · of the ¦ sea,

9 Even there your ꞁ hand shall ꞁ lead me:
and ꞁ your right ꞁ hand shall ꞁ hold me.

10 If I say 'Surely the ꞁ darkness · will ꞁ cover me:
and the ꞁ night ꞁ will enꞁclose me',

11 The darkness is no darkness with you
but the night is as ꞁ clear · as the ꞁ day:
the darkness and the ꞁ light are ꞁ both aꞁlike.

12 For you have created my ꞁ inward ꞁ parts:
you knit me together ꞁ in my ꞁ mother's ꞁ womb.

13 I will praise you for ꞁ you are · to be ꞁ feared:
fearful are your ꞁ acts and ꞁ wonderful · your ꞁ work

14 You knew my soul * and my bones were not ꞁ hidden
from you:
when I was formed in secret
and ꞁ woven · in the ꞁ depths · of the ꞁ earth.

15 Your eyes saw my limbs when they were ꞁ yet im
perfect:
and in your book were ꞁ all my ꞁ members ꞁ writte

†16 Day by ꞁ day · they were ꞁ fashioned:
and not ꞁ one was ꞁ late in ꞁ growing.

17 How deep are your thoughts to ꞁ me O ꞁ God:
and how ꞁ great ꞁ is the ꞁ sum of them!

18 Were I to count them
they are more in number ꞁ than the ꞁ sand:
were I to come to the ꞁ end · I would ꞁ still be ꞁ wit
you.

[19 If only you would slay the | wicked · O | God:
if only the men of | blood · would de|part | from me!

20 For they affront you | by their | evil:
and your enemies ex|alt them|selves a|gainst you.

21 Do I not hate them O Lord that | hate | you:
do I not loathe | those · who re|bel a|gainst you?

22 I hate them with a | perfect | hatred:
they | have be|come my | enemies.]

23 Search me out O God and | know my | heart:
put me to the | proof and | know my | thoughts.

24 Look well lest there be any way of | wicked·ness | in me:
and lead me in the | way · that is | ever|lasting.

140

1 Deliver me O Lord from | evil | men:
and pre|serve me · from | vio·lent | men,

2 Who devise mischief | in their | hearts:
who stir up | enmi·ty | day by | day.

3 They have sharpened their | tongues · like a | serpent's:
and the venom of | asps is | under · their | lips.

4 Keep me O Lord from the | power · of the | wicked:
preserve me from violent men
who think to | thrust me | from my | course.

5 The arrogant have laid a snare for me
and rogues have | stretched the | net:
they have set | traps a|long my | way.

6 But I have said to the Lord ǀ 'You are · my ǀ God':
hear O ǀ Lord the ǀ voice of · my ǀ pleading.

7 O Lord my God and my ǀ sure ǀ stronghold:
you have covered my ǀ head · in the ǀ day of ǀ battle.

8 Do not fulfil O Lord the deǀsire · of the ǀ wicked:
nor further the ǀ evil · that he ǀ has deǀvised.

[9 Let not those that beset me ǀ lift their ǀ heads:
but let the mischief that is ǀ on their ǀ lips ǀ bury them.

10 Let hot burning coals be ǀ poured upǀon them:
let them be plunged into that miry pit‿
from ǀ which · they shall ǀ never · aǀrise.

[†] 11 Let no man of evil tongue find ǀ footing · in the ǀ land:
the evil the violent man let him be ǀ hunted ǀ to the ǀ end.]

12 I know that the Lord will work justice ǀ for · the opǀpressed:
and right ǀ judgements ǀ for the ǀ poor.

13 Surely the righteous shall have cause to ǀ praise your ǀ name:
and the ǀ just shall ǀ dwell in · your ǀ sight.

141

1 O Lord I call to you make | haste to | help me:
and | hear my | voice · when I | cry.

2 Let my prayer be as | incense · be|fore you:
and the lifting up of my | hands · as the | evening |
sacrifice.

3 Set a guard O | Lord · on my | mouth:
and | keep the | door · of my | lips.

4 Let not my heart incline to evil speech
to join in wickedness with | wrong|doers:
let me not taste the | pleasures | of their | table.

5 But let the righteous | man chas|tise me:
and the | faithful | man re|buke me.

6 Let not the oil of the wicked an|oint my | head:
for I pray to you | still a|gainst their | wickedness.

7 They shall be cast down‿
by that Mighty One who | is their | judge:
and how pleasing shall my | words be | to them | then!

8 As when a farmer | breaks the | ground:
so shall their bones lie | scattered · at the | mouth of |
Sheol.

9 But my eyes look to you O | Lord my | God:
to you I come for refuge | do not · pour | out my |
life.

10 Keep me from the snare that | they have | laid for me:
and from the | traps · of the | evil|doers.

†11 Let the wicked fall together into their | own | nets:
whilst | I pass | safely | by.

142

1 I call to the Lord with a | loud | voice:
with loud | voice · I en|treat his | favour.

2 I pour out my com|plaint be|fore him:
and | tell him | all my | trouble.

3 When my spirit is faint within me you | know my | path:
in the way where I walk | ‿
they have | hidden · a | snare for me.

4 I look to my right | hand and | see:
but | no | man will | know me;

5 All es|cape is | gone:
and | there is | no one · who | cares for me.

6 I call to you O Lord   I say | 'You are · my | refuge:
you are my | portion · in the | land · of the | living.'

7 Heed my loud crying   for I am | brought · very | low:
O save me from my persecutors | ‿
for they | are too | strong for me.

8 Bring me | out of · the | prison-house:
that | I may | praise your | name.

†9 When you have given me | my re|ward:
then will the | righteous | gather · a|bout me.

143

1 Hear my | prayer O | Lord:
in your faithfulness consider my petition
and in your | righteous·ness | give me | answer.

2 Bring not your servant | into | judgement:
for in your sight can | no man | living · be | justified.

3 For the enemy has pursued me
he has crushed my | life · to the | ground:
he has made me dwell in darkness‿
like | those for | ever | dead.

4 Therefore my | spirit · grows | faint:
and my | heart · is ap|palled with|in me.

5 I remember the days of old
I think on all that | you have | done:
I con|sider · the | works of · your | hands.

6 I stretch out my | hands to|ward you:
my soul yearns for you | like a | thirsty | land.

7 Be swift to hear me O Lord   for my | spirit | fails:
hide not your face from me
lest I be like | those who · go | down · to the | Pit.

8 O let me hear of your merciful kindness in the morning
for my | trust · is in | you:
show me the way that I should go
for | you | are my | hope.

9 Deliver me from my | enemies · O | Lord:
for I | run to | you for | shelter.

10 Teach me to do your will   for | you are · my | God:
let your kindly spirit | lead me · in an | even | path.

(†) 11 For your name's sake O Lord pre¦serve my ¦ life:
and for the sake of your righteousness ¦ bring me out of ¦ trouble.

[12 In your merciful goodness slay my enemies
and destroy all those that ¦ come a¦gainst me:
for ¦ truly · I ¦ am your ¦ servant.]

144

1 Blessèd be the ¦ Lord my ¦ Rock:
who teaches my hands to ¦ war · and my ¦ fingers · to fight;

2 My strength and my stronghold
my fortress and ¦ my de¦liverer:
my shield to whom I come for refuge
who sub¦dues the ¦ peoples ¦ under me.

3 Lord what is man that you should be ¦ mindful ¦ of him:
or the son of man ¦ that you ¦ should con¦sider him?

4 Man is but a ¦ breath of ¦ wind:
his days are like a ¦ shadow · that ¦ passes · a¦way.

5 Part the heavens O Lord and ¦ come ¦ down:
touch the ¦ mountains · and ¦ they shall ¦ smoke.

6 Dart forth your lightnings
and scatter them on ¦ every ¦ side:
let loose your ¦ arrows · with the ¦ roar · of the ¦ thunderbolt.

7 Reach down your hand from on high
rescue me and pluck me out of the | great | waters:
out of the | hands | of the | aliens,

8 Whose | mouths speak | perjury:
and their right hand | is a · right | hand of | falsehood.

9 I will sing you a new | song O | God:
on the ten-stringed | lute · will I | sing your | praises.

10 You have given | victory · to | kings:
and de|liverance · to | David · your | servant.

11 O save me from the | peril · of the | sword:
pluck me out of the | hands | of the | aliens,

12 Whose | mouths speak | perjury:
and their right hand | is a · right | hand of | falsehood.

13 Our sons in their youth shall be like | sturdy | plants:
and our daughters as the | carved | corners · of | palaces.

14 Our barns shall be full and give food of | every | kind:
the sheep shall lamb in our fields‿
in | thousands · and | tens of | thousands.

15 Our cattle shall be heavy with calf
there shall be no miscarriage or un|timely | birth:
and no loud | crying | in our | streets.

16 Happy the people whose lot is | such as | this:
happy that people who | have the | Lord for · their | God!

145

1 I will exalt you O ǀ God my ǀ king:
I will bless your ǀ name for ǀ ever · and ǀ ever.

2 Every ǀ day · will I ǀ bless you:
and praise your ǀ name for ǀ ever · and ǀ ever.

3 Great is the Lord * and wonderfully ǀ worthy · to be ǀ praised:
his greatness is ǀ past ǀ searching ǀ out.

4 One generation shall praise your ǀ works · to anǀother:
and deǀclare your ǀ mighty ǀ acts.

5 As for me * I will be talking‿
of the glorious splendour ǀ of your ǀ majesty:
I will tell the ǀ story · of your ǀ marvel·lous ǀ works.

6 Men shall recount the power of your ǀ terri·ble ǀ deeds:
and ǀ I will · proǀclaim your ǀ greatness.

†7 Their lips shall flow‿
with the remembrance of your aǀbundant ǀ goodness:
they shall ǀ shout for ǀ joy at · your ǀ righteousness.

8 The Lord is ǀ gracious · and comǀpassionate:
slow to anger ǀ and of ǀ great ǀ goodness.

9 The Lord is ǀ loving · to ǀ every man:
and his mercy is ǀ over ǀ all his ǀ works.

10 All creation ǀ praises you · O ǀ Lord:
and your faithful ǀ servants ǀ bless your ǀ name.

11 They speak of the glory ǀ of your ǀ kingdom:
and ǀ tell of · your ǀ great ǀ might,

†12 That all mankind may know your | mighty | acts:
and the glorious | splendour | of your | kingdom.

13 Your kingdom is an ever|lasting | kingdom:
and your dominion en|dures through | all · gener|a-
tions.

14 The Lord upholds all | those who | stumble:
and raises up | those · that are | bowed | down.

15 The eyes of all look to | you in | hope:
and you give them their | food in | due | season;

16 You open | wide your | hand:
and fill all things | living · with your | bounte·ous | gift.

17 The Lord is just in | all his | ways:
and | faithful · in | all his | dealings.

18 The Lord is near to all who | call up|on him:
to all who | call up|on him · in | truth.

19 He will fulfil the desire of | those that | fear him:
he will | hear their | cry and | save them.

20 The Lord preserves all | those that | love him:
but the wicked | he will | utterly · de|stroy.

†21 My mouth shall speak the | praises · of the | Lord:
and let all flesh bless his holy | name
for | ever · and | ever.

146

1 Praise the Lord
praise the Lord | O my | soul:
while I | live · I will | praise the | Lord;

2 While I | have · any | being:
I will sing | praises | to my | God.

3 Put not your | trust in | princes:
nor in the sons of | men who | cannot | save.

4 For when their breath goes from them
they return a|gain · to the | earth:
and on that day | all their | thoughts | perish.

5 Blessèd is the man whose help is the | God of | Jacob:
whose hope is | in the | Lord his | God,

6 The God who made | heaven · and | earth:
the sea and | all | that is | in them,

†7 Who keeps | faith for | ever:
who deals justice to | those that | are op|pressed.

8 The Lord gives | food · to the | hungry:
and | sets the | captives | free.

9 The Lord gives | sight · to the | blind:
the Lord lifts up | those · that are | bowed | down.

10 The Lord | loves the | righteous:
the Lord cares for the | stranger | in the | land.

11 He upholds the | widow · and the | fatherless:
as for the way of the wicked he | turns it | upside|
down.

12 The Lord shall be ǀ king for ǀ ever:
your God O Zion shall reign through all generations ǀ
Praise ǀ – the ǀ Lord.

147

1 O praise the Lord
for it is good to sing praises ǀ to our ǀ God:
and to ǀ praise him · is ǀ joyful · and ǀ right.

2 The Lord is reǀbuilding · Jeǀrusalem:
he is gathering together‿
the ǀ scattered ǀ outcasts · of ǀ Israel.

3 He heals the ǀ broken · in ǀ spirit:
and ǀ binds ǀ up their ǀ wounds.

4 He counts the ǀ number · of the ǀ stars:
and ǀ calls them ǀ all by ǀ name.

5 Great is our Lord and ǀ great · is his ǀ power:
there is no ǀ measuring · his ǀ underǀstanding.

6 The Lord reǀstores the ǀ humble:
but he brings down the ǀ wicked ǀ to the ǀ dust.

7 O sing to the Lord a ǀ song of ǀ thanksgiving:
sing praises to our ǀ God upǀon the ǀ harp.

8 He covers the heavens with cloud
and prepares ǀ rain · for the ǀ earth:
and makes the grass to ǀ sprout upǀon the ǀ mountains.

9 He gives the ǀ cattle · their ǀ food:
and feeds the young ǀ ravens · that ǀ call ǀ to him.

10 He takes no pleasure in the | strength · of a | horse:
nor does he de|light in | any · man's | legs,

†11 But the Lord's delight is in | those that | fear him:
who | wait in | hope · for his | mercy.

12 Praise the | Lord · O Je|rusalem:
sing | praises · to your | God O | Zion.

13 For he has strengthened the | bars of · your | gates:
and | blessed your | children · with|in you.

14 He makes peace with|in your | borders:
and satisfies you | with the | finest | wheat.

15 He sends his com|mand · to the | earth:
and his | word runs | very | swiftly.

16 He gives | snow like | wool:
and | scatters · the | hoar-frost · like | ashes.

17 He sprinkles his ice like | morsels · of | bread:
and the waters | harden | at his | frost.

†18 He sends out his | word and | melts them:
he blows with his | wind · and the | waters | flow.

19 He made his word | known to | Jacob:
his | statutes · and | judgements · to | Israel.

20 He has not dealt so with any | other | nation:
nor have they knowledge of his laws |
Praise | – the | Lord.

148

1 Praise the Lord
praise the ˈ Lord from ˈ heaven:
O ˈ praise him ˈ in the ˈ heights.

2 Praise him ˈ all his ˈ angels:
O ˈ praise him ˈ all his ˈ host.

3 Praise him ˈ sun and ˈ moon:
praise him ˈ all you ˈ stars of ˈ light.

4 Praise him you ˈ highest ˈ heaven:
and you waters that ˈ are aˈbove the ˈ heavens.

5 Let them praise the ˈ name · of the ˈ Lord:
for he comˈmanded · and ˈ they were ˈ made.

6 He established them for ˈ ever · and ˈ ever:
he made an ordinance which ˈ shall not ˈ pass aˈway.

7 O praise the ˈ Lord · from the ˈ earth:
praise him you sea-ˈmonsters · and ˈ all ˈ deeps;

8 Fire and hail ˈ mist and ˈ snow:
and storm-wind fulˈfilling ˈ his comˈmand;

9 Mountains and ˈ all ˈ hills:
fruiting ˈ trees and ˈ all ˈ cedars;

10 Beasts of the wild and ˈ all ˈ cattle:
creeping ˈ things and ˈ winged ˈ birds;

11 Kings of the earth and ˈ all ˈ peoples:
princes and all ˈ rulers ˈ of the ˈ world;

12 Young ˡ men and ˡ maidens:
old ˡ men and ˡ children · toˡgether.

13 Let them praise the ˡ name · of the ˡ Lord:
for ˡ his · name aˡlone · is exˡalted.

14 His glory is above ˡ earth and ˡ heaven:
and he has lifted ˡ high the ˡ horn · of his ˡ people.

†15 Therefore he is the praise of ˡ all his ˡ servants:
of the children of Israel a people that is near him ˡ
Praise ˡ – the ˡ Lord.

149

1 O praise the Lord
and sing to the Lord a ˡ new ˡ song:
O praise him in the asˡsembly ˡ of the ˡ faithful.

2 Let Israel rejoice in ˡ him that ˡ made him:
let the children of Zion be ˡ joyful ˡ in their ˡ king.

3 Let them praise him ˡ in the ˡ dance:
let them sing his praise with ˡ timbrel ˡ and with ˡ
harp.

4 For the Lord takes deˡlight · in his ˡ people:
he adorns the ˡ meek with ˡ his salˡvation.

5 Let his faithful ones exˡult · in his ˡ glory:
let them sing for ˡ joy upˡon their ˡ beds.

6 Let the high praises of God be ˡ in their ˡ mouths:
and a ˡ two-edged ˡ sword · in their ˡ hands,

7 To execute vengeance | on the | nations;
and | chastisement · up|on the | peoples,

8 To bind their | kings in | chains:
and their | nobles · with | fetters · of | iron,

†9 To visit upon them the judgement that | is de|creed:
such honour belongs to all his faithful servants |
Praise | – the | Lord.

150

1 Praise the Lord
O praise | God · in his | sanctuary:
praise him in the | firma·ment | of his | power.

2 Praise him for his | mighty | acts:
praise him according to | his a|bundant | goodness.

3 Praise him in the | blast · of the | ram's horn:
praise him up|on the | lute and | harp.

4 Praise him with the | timbrel · and | dances:
praise him up|on the | strings and | pipe.

5 Praise him on the | high-·sounding | cymbals:
praise him up|on the | loud | cymbals.

6 Let everything that has breath | praise the | Lord:
O | praise | – the | Lord!